Learning Kibana 7
Second Edition

Build powerful Elastic dashboards with Kibana's data
visualization capabilities

Anurag Srivastava
Bahaaldine Azarmi

BIRMINGHAM - MUMBAI

Learning Kibana 7
Second Edition

Commissioning Editor: Amey Varangaonkar
Acquisition Editor: Nelson Morris
Content Development Editors: Pratik Andrade, Anugraha Arunagiri
Senior Editor: Ayaan Hoda
Technical Editor: Snehal Dalmet, Dinesh Pawar
Copy Editor: Safis Editing
Project Coordinator: Vaidehi Sawant
Proofreader: Safis Editing
Indexer: Manju Arasan
Production Designer: Deepika Naik

First published: February 2017
Second edition: July 2019

Production reference: 1190719

Published by Packt Publishing Ltd.
Livery Place
35 Livery Street
Birmingham
B3 2PB, UK.

ISBN 978-1-83855-036-3

www.packtpub.com

To my mom; my dad; my wife, Chanchal; and my son, Anvit.

– Anurag Srivastava

Packt.com

Subscribe to our online digital library for full access to over 7,000 books and videos, as well as industry leading tools to help you plan your personal development and advance your career. For more information, please visit our website.

Why subscribe?

- Spend less time learning and more time coding with practical eBooks and Videos from over 4,000 industry professionals

- Improve your learning with Skill Plans built especially for you

- Get a free eBook or video every month

- Fully searchable for easy access to vital information

- Copy and paste, print, and bookmark content

Did you know that Packt offers eBook versions of every book published, with PDF and ePub files available? You can upgrade to the eBook version at www.packt.com and as a print book customer, you are entitled to a discount on the eBook copy. Get in touch with us at customercare@packtpub.com for more details.

At www.packt.com, you can also read a collection of free technical articles, sign up for a range of free newsletters, and receive exclusive discounts and offers on Packt books and eBooks.

Contributors

About the authors

Anurag Srivastava is a senior technical lead in a multinational software company. He has more than 12 years' experience in web-based application development. He is proficient in designing architecture for scalable and highly available applications. He has handled dev teams and multiple clients from all over the globe over the past 10 years of his professional career. He has significant experience with the Elastic Stack (Elasticsearch, Logstash, and Kibana) for creating dashboards using system metrics data, log data, application data, or relational databases. He has authored other two books—*Mastering Kibana 6.x*, and *Kibana 7 Quick Start Guide*, both published by Packt.

Bahaaldine Azarmi, or Baha for short, is the head of solutions architecture in the EMEA South region at Elastic. Prior to this position, Baha co-founded ReachFive, a marketing data platform focused on user behavior and social analytics. He has also worked for a number of different software vendors, including Talend and Oracle, where he held positions as a solutions architect and architect. Prior to *Machine Learning with the Elastic Stack*, Baha authored books including *Learning Kibana 5.0*, *Scalable Big Data Architecture*, and *Talend for Big Data*. He is based in Paris and holds an MSc in computer science from Polytech'Paris.

About the reviewer

Giacomo Veneri graduated in computer science from the University of Siena. He holds a PhD in neuroscience, along with having various scientific publications to his name. He is Predix IoT-certified and an influencer, as well as being certified in SCRUM and Oracle Java. He has 20 years' experience as an IT architect and team leader. He has been an expert on IoT in the fields of oil and gas and transportation since 2013. He lives in Tuscany, where he loves cycling. He is also the author of *Hands-On Industrial Internet of Things* and *Maven Build Customization*, both published by Packt.

Packt is searching for authors like you

If you're interested in becoming an author for Packt, please visit authors.packtpub.com and apply today. We have worked with thousands of developers and tech professionals, just like you, to help them share their insight with the global tech community. You can make a general application, apply for a specific hot topic that we are recruiting an author for, or submit your own idea.

Table of Contents

Preface

This book is here to help you understand the core concepts and the practical implementation of Kibana in different use cases. It covers how to ingest data from different sources into Elasticsearch using Beats or Logstash. It then shows how to explore, analyze, and visualize the data in Kibana. This book covers how to play with time series data to create complex graphs using Timelion and show them along with other visualizations on your dashboard, then how to embed your dashboard or visualization on a web page. You will also learn how to use APM to monitor your application by installing and configuring the APM server and APM agents. We will explore how Canvas can be used to create awesome visualizations. We will also cover different X-Pack features such as user and role management in security, alerting, monitoring, and machine learning. This book will also explain how to create machine learning jobs to find anomalies in your data.

Who this book is for

Aspiring Elastic developers, data analysts, and those interested in learning about the new features of Kibana 7 will find this book very useful. No prior knowledge of Kibana is expected. Previous experience with Elasticsearch will help, but is not mandatory.

What this book covers

Chapter 1, *Understanding Your Data for Kibana*, introduces the notion of data drive architecture by explaining the main challenges in the industry, how the Elastic Stack is structured, and what data we'll use to implement some of the use cases in Kibana.

Chapter 2, *Installing and Setting Up Kibana*, walks the reader through the installation of the Elastic Stack on different platforms.

Chapter 3, *Business Analytics with Kibana*, describes what a business analytics use case is through a real-life example, and then walks the reader through the process of data ingestion.

Chapter 4, *Data Visualization Using Kibana*, describes visualization and dashboarding. The readers will learn how to create different visualizations, before moving on to how to create a dashboard using these visualizations.

Chapter 5, *Dev Tools and Timelion,* is focused on Dev Tools and Timelion in Kibana. The readers will learn different options of Dev Tools, such as using Console to run Elasticsearch queries right from the Kibana interface. Then we will cover using Search Profiler to profile the Elasticsearch queries, and using Grok Debugger to create a Grok pattern with which we can convert unstructured data into structured data through Logstash. After that, we will cover Timelion, with which we can play with time-series data, because it provides some functions that can be chained together to create a complex visualization for specific use cases that can't be created using the Kibana Visualize option.

Chapter 6, *Space and Graph Exploration in Kibana,* describes the Elastic Stack Graph plugin, which provides graph analytics. The reader will be walked through the main use cases that the Graph plugin tries to solve, and will see how to interact with the data. After that, we will cover how to create different Spaces and add them with different roles and users.

Chapter 7, *Elastic Stack Features,* describes the importance of Elastic features. We will cover security using user and role management, and will then cover reporting, with which we can export CSV and PDF reports. After that, we will explore how to use monitoring to monitor the complete Elastic Stack, and with Watcher, we will configure the alerting system to send an email whenever a value crosses a specified threshold.

Chapter 8, *Kibana Canvas and Plugins,* describes the Kibana Canvas and explains how we can create custom dashboards with it.

Chapter 9, *Application Performance Monitoring,* describes **Application Performance Monitoring (APM)** and how it can be configured to monitor an application. We will cover the installation of APM Server and configure it to receive data from APM agents. Then, we will cover the installation and configuration of APM agents with the application in order to fetch the application data. Lastly, we will explain how to explore data with the built-in APM UI or Kibana Dashboard.

Chapter 10, *Machine Learning with Kibana,* introduces machine learning and explores how to find data anomalies and predict future trends.

To get the most out of this book

In this book, you will need to download and install the Elastic Stack, specifically, Elasticsearch, Kibana, Beats, Logstash, and APM. All the software is available from http://www.elastic.co/downloads. The Elastic Stack can be run on various environments on different machines and setups. The support matrix is available at https://www.elastic.co/support/matrix.

Download the example code files

You can download the example code files for this book from your account at `www.packt.com`. If you purchased this book elsewhere, you can visit `www.packt.com/support` and register to have the files emailed directly to you.

You can download the code files by following these steps:

1. Log in or register at `www.packt.com`.
2. Select the **SUPPORT** tab.
3. Click on **Code Downloads & Errata**.
4. Enter the name of the book in the **Search** box and follow the onscreen instructions.

Once the file is downloaded, please make sure that you unzip or extract the folder using the latest version of:

- WinRAR/7-Zip for Windows
- Zipeg/iZip/UnRarX for Mac
- 7-Zip/PeaZip for Linux

The code bundle for the book is also hosted on GitHub at `https://github.com/PacktPublishing/Learning-Kibana-7-Second-Edition`. In case there's an update to the code, it will be updated on the existing GitHub repository.

We also have other code bundles from our rich catalog of books and videos available at `https://github.com/PacktPublishing/`. Check them out!

Download the color images

We also provide a PDF file that has color images of the screenshots/diagrams used in this book. You can download it here: `https://static.packt-cdn.com/downloads/9781838550363_ColorImages.pdf`.

Conventions used

There are a number of text conventions used throughout this book.

`CodeInText`: Indicates code words in text, database table names, folder names, filenames, file extensions, pathnames, dummy URLs, user input, and Twitter handles. Here is an example: "For CentOS and older Red Hat-based distributions, we can use the `yum` command".

A block of code is set as follows:

```
input {
    file {
        path => "/home/user/Downloads/Popular_Baby_Names.csv"
        start_position => beginning
    }
}
```

When we wish to draw your attention to a particular part of a code block, the relevant lines or items are set in bold:

```
elasticsearch {
        action => "index"
        hosts => ["127.0.0.1:9200"]
        index => "Popular_Baby_Names"
}
```

Any command-line input or output is written as follows:

```
unzip elasticsearch-7.1.0-windows-x86_64.zip
cd elasticsearch-7.1.0/
```

Bold: Indicates a new term, an important word, or words that you see onscreen. For example, words in menus or dialog boxes appear in the text like this. Here is an example: "Now, we need to click on the **Next step** button."

Warnings or important notes appear like this.

Tips and tricks appear like this.

Get in touch

Feedback from our readers is always welcome.

General feedback: If you have questions about any aspect of this book, mention the book title in the subject of your message and email us at customercare@packtpub.com.

Errata: Although we have taken every care to ensure the accuracy of our content, mistakes do happen. If you have found a mistake in this book, we would be grateful if you would report this to us. Please visit www.packt.com/submit-errata, selecting your book, clicking on the Errata Submission Form link, and entering the details.

Piracy: If you come across any illegal copies of our works in any form on the Internet, we would be grateful if you would provide us with the location address or website name. Please contact us at copyright@packt.com with a link to the material.

If you are interested in becoming an author: If there is a topic that you have expertise in and you are interested in either writing or contributing to a book, please visit authors.packtpub.com.

Reviews

Please leave a review. Once you have read and used this book, why not leave a review on the site that you purchased it from? Potential readers can then see and use your unbiased opinion to make purchase decisions, we at Packt can understand what you think about our products, and our authors can see your feedback on their book. Thank you!

For more information about Packt, please visit packt.com.

Section 1: Understanding Kibana 7

In this section, we will start with a basic introduction to the Elastic Stack and then discuss what's new in Elastic Stack 7. We will then cover the installation process of the Elastic Stack. By the end of this section, we will know how we can create an index pattern in Kibana.

The following chapters will be covered in this section:

- Chapter 1, *Understanding Your Data for Kibana*
- Chapter 2, *Installing and Setting Up Kibana*

Understanding Your Data for Kibana

We are living in a digital world in which data is growing at an exponential rate; every digital device sends data on a regular basis and it is continuously being stored. Now, storing huge amounts of data is not a problem—we can use cheap hard drives to store as much data as we want. But the most important thing that we can do with that data is to get the information that we need or want out of it. Once we understand our data, we can then analyze or visualize it. This data can be from any domain, such as accounting, infrastructure, healthcare, business, medical, **Internet of Things (IoT)**, and more, and it can be structured or unstructured. The main challenge for any organization is to first understand the data they are storing, analyze it to get the information they need, create visualizations, and, from this, gain an insight of the data in a visual format that is easy to understand and enables people in management roles to take quick decisions.

However, it can be difficult to fetch information from data due to the following reasons:

- **Data brings complexity**: It is not easy to get to the root cause of any issue; for example, let's say that we want to find out why the traffic system of a city behaves badly on certain days of a month. This issue could be dependent on another set of data that we may not be monitoring. In this case, we could get a better understanding by checking the weather report data for the month. We can then try and find any correlations between the data and discover a pattern.

- **Data comes from different sources**: As I have already mentioned, one dataset can depend on another dataset and they can come from two different sources. Now, there may be instances where we cannot get access to all the data sources that are dependent on each other and, for these situations, it is important to understand and gather data from other sources and not just the one that you are interested in.

- **Data is growing at a faster pace**: As we move toward a digital era, we are capturing more and more data. As data grows at a quicker pace, it also creates issues in terms of what to keep, how to keep it, and how to process such huge amounts of data to get the relevant information that we need from it.

We can solve these issues by using the Elastic Stack, as we can store data from different sources by pushing it to Elasticsearch and then analyzing and visualizing it in Kibana. Kibana solves many data analysis issues as it provides many features that allow us to play around with the data, and we can also do a lot of things with it. In this book, we will cover all of these features and try to cover their practical implementation as well.

In this chapter, we will cover the following topics:

- Data analysis and visualization challenges for industries
- Understanding your data for analysis in Kibana
- Limitations with existing tools
- Components of the Elastic Stack

Industry challenges

Depending on the industry, the use cases can be very different in terms of data usage. In any given industry, data is used in different ways and for different purposes—whether it's for security analytics or order management. Data comes in various formats and different scales of volumes. In the telecommunications industry, for example, it's very common to see projects about the quality of services where data is taken from 100,000 network devices.

The challenge for these industries is to handle the huge quantities of data and to get real-time visualizations from which decisions can be taken. Data capture is usually performed for applications, but to utilize this data for creating a real-time dashboard is a challenge. For that, Kibana can be used, along with Beats and Logstash, to push data from different sources, Elasticsearch can be used to store that data, and then, finally, Kibana can be used to analyze and visualize it. So, if we summarize the industry issue, it has the same canonical issues as the following:

- How to handle huge quantities of data as this comes with a lot of complexity
- How to visualize data effectively and in a real-time fashion so that we can get data insights easily

Once this is achieved, we can easily recognize the visual patterns in data and, based on that, we can derive the information out of it that we need without dealing with the burden of exploring tons of data. So, let me now explain a real scenario that will help you to understand the actual challenge of data capture. I will take a simple use case to explain the issues and will then explain the technologies that can be used to solve them.

Use cases to explain industry issues

If we consider the ways in which we receive huge amounts of data, then you will note that there are many different sources that we can use to get structured or unstructured data. In this digital world, we use many devices that keep on generating and sending data to a central server where the data is then stored. For instance, the applications that we access generate data, the smartphones or smartwatches we use generate data, and even the cab services, railways, and air travel systems we use for transportation all generate data.

A system and its running processes also generate data, and so, in this way, there are many different ways in which we can get data. We get this data at regular intervals and it either accumulates on the physical drive of a computer or, more frequently, it can be hidden within data centers that are hard to fetch and explore. In order to explore this data and to analyze it, we need to extract (**ship**) it from different locations (such as from log files, databases, or applications), convert it from an unstructured data format into a structured data format (**transform**), and then push the transformed data into a central place (**store**) where we can access it for analysis. This flow of data streaming in the system requires a proper architecture to be shipped, transformed, stored, and accessed in a scalable and distributed way.

End users, driven by the need to process increasingly higher volumes of data while maintaining real-time query responses, have turned away from more traditional, relational database or data warehousing solutions, due to poor scalability or performance. The solution is increasingly found in highly distributed, clustered data stores that can easily be monitored. Let's take the example of application monitoring, which is one of the most common use cases we meet across industries. Each application logs data, sometimes in a centralized way (for example, by using syslog), and sometimes all the logs are spread out across the infrastructure, which makes it hard to have a single point of access to the data stream.

The majority of large organizations don't retain logged data for longer than the duration of a log file rotation (that is, a few hours or even minutes). This means that, by the time an issue has occurred, the data that could provide the answers is lost.

So, when you actually have the data, what do you do? Well, there are different ways to extract the gist of logs. A lot of people start by using a simple string pattern search (GREP). Essentially, they try to find matching patterns in logs using a regular expression. That might work for a single log file but, if you want to search something from different log files, then you need to open individual log files for each date to apply the regular expression.

GREP is convenient but, clearly, it doesn't fit our need to react quickly to failure in order to reduce the **Mean Time To Recovery (MTTR)**. Think about it: what if we were talking about a major issue in the purchasing API of an e-commerce website? What if the users experience a high latency on this page or, worse, can't go to the end of the purchase process? The time you will spend trying to recover your application from gigabytes of logs is money you could potentially lose. Another potential issue could be around a lack of security analytics and not being able to blacklist the IPs that try to brute force your application.

In the same context, I've seen use cases where people didn't know that every night there was a group of IPs attempting to get into their system, and this was just because they were not able to visualize the IPs on a map and trigger alerts based on their value. A simple, yet very effective, pattern in order to protect the system would have been to limit access to resources or services to the internal system only. The ability to whitelist access to a known set of IP addresses is essential. The consequence could be dramatic if a proper data-driven architecture with a solid visualization layer is not serving those needs. For example, it could lead to a lack of visibility and control, an increase in the MTTR, customer dissatisfaction, financial impact, security leaks, and bad response times and user experiences.

Understanding your data for analysis in Kibana

Here, we will discuss different aspects of data analysis such as data shipping, data ingestion, data storage, and data visualization. These are all very important aspects of data analysis and visualization, and we need to understand each of them in detail. The objective is to then understand how to avoid any confusion, and build an architecture that will serve the different following aspects.

Data shipping

Data-shipping architecture should support any sort of data or event transport that is either structured or unstructured. The primary goal of data shipping is to send data from remote machines to a centralized location in order to make it available for further exploration. For data shipping, we generally deploy lightweight agents that sit on the same server from where we want to get the data. These shippers fetch the data and keep on sending them to the centralized server. For data shipping, we need to consider the following:

- The agents should be lightweight. They should not take resources with the process that generates the actual data, in order to minimize the performance impact and place fewer footprints on it.
- There are a lot of data shipping technologies out there; some of them are tied to a specific technology, while others are based on an extensible framework that can adapt relatively to a data source.
- Shipping data is not only about sending data over the wire; in fact, it's also about security and making sure that the data is sent to the proper destination with an end-to-end secured pipeline.
- Another aspect of data shipping is the management of data loads. Shipping data should be done relative to the load that the end destination is able to ingest; this feature is called **back pressure management**.

It's essential for data visualization to rely on reliable data shipping. As an example, consider data flowing from financial trade machines and how critical it could be not to be able to detect a security leak just because you are losing data.

Data ingestion

The scope of an ingestion layer is to receive data, encompassing as wide a range of commonly used transport protocols and data formats as possible, while providing capabilities to extract and transform this data before finally storing it.

Processing data can somehow be seen as **extracting, transforming,** and **loading** (ETL) data, which is often called an **ingestion pipeline** and, essentially, receives data from the shipping layer to push it to a storage layer. It comes with the following features:

- Generally, the ingestion layer has a pluggable architecture to ease integration with the various sources of data and destinations, with the help of a set of plugins. Some of the plugins are made for receiving data from shippers, which means that data is not always received from shippers and can come directly from a data source such as a file, a network, or even a database. It can be ambiguous in some cases: should I use a shipper or a pipeline to ingest data from the file? It will, of course, depend on the use case and also on the expected SLAs.

- The ingestion layer should be used to prepare the data by, for example, parsing the data, formatting the data, doing the correlation with other data sources, and normalizing and enriching the data before storage. This has many advantages, but the most important advantage is that it can improve the quality of the data, providing better insights for visualization. Another advantage could be to remove processing overheads later on, by precomputing a value or looking up a reference. The drawback of this is that you may need to ingest the data again if the data is not properly formatted or enriched for visualization. Hopefully, there are some ways to process the data after it has been ingested.

- Ingesting and transforming data consumes compute resources. It is essential that we consider this, usually in terms of maximum data throughput per unit, and plan for ingestion by distributing the load over multiple ingestion instances. This is a very important aspect of real-time visualization, or, to be precise, near real-time visualization. If ingestion is spread across multiple instances, it can accelerate the storage of the data and, therefore, make it available faster for visualization.

Storing data at scale

Storage is undoubtedly the masterpiece of the data-driven architecture. It provides the essential, long-term retention of your data. It also provides the core functionality to search, analyze, and discover insights in your data. It is the heart of the process. The action will depend on the nature of the technology. Here are some aspects that the storage layer usually brings:

- Scalability is the main aspect, that is, the storage used for various volumes of data that could start from gigabytes to terabytes to petabytes of data. The scalability is horizontal, which means that, as demand and volume grow, you should be able to increase the capacity of the storage seamlessly by adding more machines.

- Most of the time, a non-relational and highly distributed data store, which allows fast data access and analysis at a high volume and on a variety of data types, is used, namely, a NoSQL data store. Data is partitioned and spread over a set of machines in order to balance the load while reading or writing data.

- For data visualization, it's essential that the storage exposes an API to make analysis on top of the data. Letting the visualization layer do the statistical analysis, such as grouping data over a given dimension (**aggregation**), wouldn't scale.

- The nature of the API can depend on the expectation of the visualization layer, but most of the time it's about aggregations. The visualization should only render the result of the heavy lifting done at the storage level.

- A data-driven architecture can serve data to a lot of different applications and users, and for different levels of SLAs. High availability becomes the norm in such architectures, and, like scalability, it should be part of the nature of the solution.

Visualizing data

The visualization layer is the window on the data. It provides a set of tools to build live graphs and charts to bring the data to life, allowing you to build rich, insightful dashboards that answer the questions: *What is happening now? Is my business healthy? What is the mood of the market?*

The visualization layer in a data-driven architecture is a layer where we expect the majority of the data consumption and is mostly focused on bringing KPIs on top of stored data. It comes with the following essential features:

- It should be lightweight and only render the result of the processing done in the storage layer
- It allows the user to discover the data and get quick out-of-the-box insights on the data
- It offers a visual way to ask unexpected questions to the data, rather than having to implement the proper request to do that
- In modern data architectures that must address the needs of accessing KPIs as fast as possible, the visualization layer should render the data in near real time
- The visualization framework should be extensible and allow users to customize the existing assets or to add new features depending on the need
- The user should be able to share the dashboards outside of the visualization application

As you can see, it's not only a matter of visualization. You need some foundations to reach the objectives. This is how we'll address the use of Kibana in this book: we'll focus on use cases and see what is the best way to leverage Kibana features, depending on the use case and context.

The main differentiator from the other visualization tools is that Kibana comes alongside a full stack, the Elastic Stack, with seamless integration with every layer of the stack, which just eases the deployment of such architecture. There are a lot of other technologies out there; we'll now explore what they are good at and what their limits are.

Technology limitations

In this section, we will try to analyze why some technologies have limitations and are not able to support end-to-end solutions for a given problem when we try to fulfill the expectations of a data-driven architecture. In these situations, either we use a set of tools to fulfill the requirement or we make certain compromises with the requirement as per the feature availability of that technology. So, let's now discuss some of the available technologies.

Relational databases

Relational databases are popular and important tools that people use to store their data in the context of a data-driven architecture; for example, we can save the application monitoring logs in a database such as MySQL that can later be used to monitor the application. But when it comes to data visualization, it starts to break all the essential features we mentioned earlier:

- A **Relational Database Management System (RDBMS)** only manages fixed schemas and is not designed to deal with dynamic data models and unstructured data. Any structural changes made on the data will require updating the schema/tables, which, as everybody knows, is expensive.
- RDBMS doesn't allow real-time data access at scale. It wouldn't be realistic, for example, to create an index for each column, for each table, or for each schema in an RDBMS; however, essentially, that is what would be required for real-time access.
- Scalability is not the easiest thing for RDBMSes; it can be a complex and heavy process to put in place and wouldn't scale against a data explosion.

RDBMSes should be used as a source of data that can be used before ingestion time in order to correlate or enrich the ingested data to have a better granularity in the visualized data. Visualization is about providing users with the flexibility to create multiple views of the data, and enabling them to explore and ask their own questions without predefining a schema or constructing a view in the storage layer.

Hadoop

The Hadoop ecosystem is pretty rich in terms of projects. It's often hard to pick or understand which project will fit our requirements; if we step back, we can consider the following aspects that Hadoop fulfills:

- It fits for massive-scale data architecture and will help to store and process any kind of data, and for any level of volume
- It has out-of-the-box batch and streaming technologies that will help to process the data as it comes in to create an iterative view on top of the raw data, or enable longer processing for larger-scale views

- The underlying architecture is made to make the integration of processing engines easy, so you can plug and process your data with a lot of different frameworks
- It's made to implement the data lake paradigms where you can essentially drop in data in order to process it

But what about visualization? Well, there are tons of initiatives out there, but the problem is that none of them can go against the real nature of Hadoop, which doesn't help for real-time data visualization at scale:

- The **Hadoop Distributed File System** (**HDFS**) is a sequential read-and-write filesystem that doesn't help for random access.
- Even the interactive ad hoc query or the existing real-time API doesn't scale in terms of integration with the visualization application. Most of the time, the user has to export their data outside of Hadoop in order to visualize it; some visualizations claim to have a transparent integration with HDFS, whereas, under the hood, the data is exported and loaded in the memory in batches, which makes the user experience pretty heavy and slow.
- Data visualization is all about APIs and easy access to the data, which Hadoop is not good at, as it always requires implementation from the user.

Hadoop is good for processing data, and is often used conjointly with other real-time technology, such as Elastic, to build Lambda architectures, as shown in the following diagram:

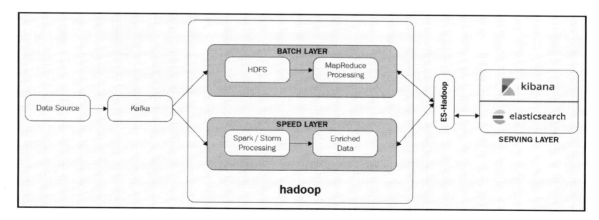

In this architecture, you can see that Hadoop aggregates incoming data either in a long processing zone or a near real-time zone. Finally, the results are indexed in **Elasticsearch** in order to be visualized in **Kibana**. Essentially, this means that one technology is not meant to replace the other, but that you can leverage the best of both.

NoSQL

There are many different, very performant, and massively scalable NoSQL technologies out there, such as key-value stores, document stores, and columnar stores; however, most of them do not serve analytic APIs or come with an out-of-the-box visualization application.

In most cases, the data that these technologies are using is ingested in an indexation engine, such as Elasticsearch, to provide analytics capabilities for visualization or search purposes.

With the fundamental layers that a data-driven architecture should have and the limits identified in existing technologies in the market, let's now introduce the Elastic Stack, which essentially answers these shortcomings.

Components of the Elastic Stack

The Elastic Stack, formerly called ELK, provides the different layers that are needed to implement a data-driven architecture.

It starts from the ingestion layer with **Beats**, **Logstash**, and the ES-Hadoop connector, then to a distributed data store with **Elasticsearch**, and, finally, to the visualization layer with **Kibana**, as shown in the following diagram:

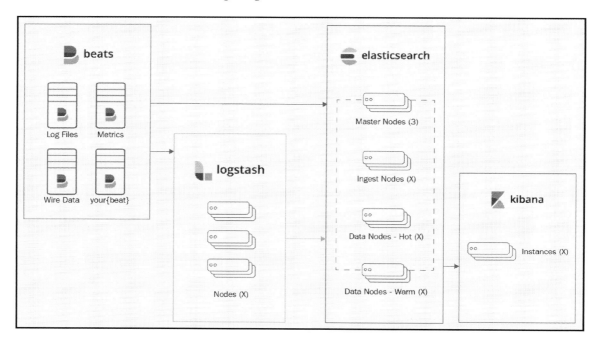

As we can see in the preceding diagram, Kibana is just one component of it.

In the following chapters, we'll focus in detail on how to use Kibana in different contexts, but we'll always need the other components. That's why you will need to understand the roles of each of them in this chapter.

One other important thing to note is that this book intends to describe how to use Kibana 7.0; therefore, in this book, we'll use Elastic Stack 7.0.0 (`https://www.elastic.co/blog/elastic-stack-7-0-0-released`).

Elasticsearch

Elasticsearch is a distributed and scalable data store from which Kibana will pull out all the aggregation results that are used in the visualization. It's resilient by nature and is designed to scale out, which means that nodes can be added to an Elasticsearch cluster depending on the needs, in a very simple way.

Elasticsearch is a highly available technology, which means the following:

- First, data is replicated across the cluster so that if there is a failure, then there is still at least one copy of the data
- Secondly, thanks to its distributed nature, Elasticsearch can spread the indexing and searching load over the cluster nodes, to ensure service continuity and respect to your SLAs

It can deal with structured and unstructured data, and, as we visualize data in Kibana, you will notice that data, or documents to use Elastic vocabulary, are indexed in the form of JSON documents. JSON makes it very handy to deal with complex data structures as it supports nested documents, arrays, and more.

Elasticsearch is a developer-friendly solution and offers a large set of REST APIs to interact with the data, or the settings of the cluster itself. The documentation for these APIs can be found at https://www.elastic.co/guide/en/elasticsearch/reference/current/docs.html.

The parts that will be interesting for this book are mainly aggregations and graphs, which will be used to make analytics on top of the indexed data (https://www.elastic.co/guide/en/elasticsearch/reference/current/search-aggregations.html) and create relationships between documents (https://www.elastic.co/guide/en/graph/current/graph-api-rest.html).

On top of these APIs, there are also client APIs that allow Elasticsearch to be integrated with most technologies such as Java, Python, Go, and more (https://www.elastic.co/guide/en/elasticsearch/client/index.html.).

Kibana generates the requests made to the cluster for each visualization. We'll examine, in this book, how to dig into it and what features and APIs have been used.

The final main aspect for Elasticsearch is that it's a real-time technology that allows working with all ranges of volumes, from gigabytes to petabytes, with the different APIs.

Besides Kibana, there are a lot of different solutions that can leverage the open APIs that Elasticsearch offers to build visualization on top of the data; however, Kibana is the only technology that is dedicated to it.

Beats

Beats is a lightweight data shipper that transports data from different sources such as applications, machines, or networks. We can install and configure Beats on any server to start receiving data. The following diagram shows how we can get data from different servers:

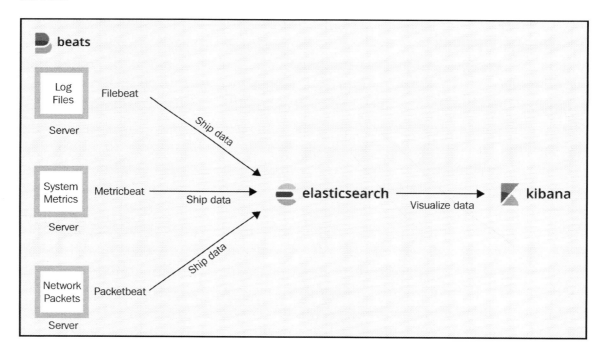

In the preceding diagram, we can see that **Filebeat**, **Metricbeat**, and **Packetbeat** send data to Elasticsearch, and this is then sent to **Kibana** for analysis or visualization. Note that we can also send data to Logstash from Beats if we want any sort of transformation of the data before sending it to Elasticsearch. Beats is built on top of **libbeat**, which is an open source library that allows every flavor of Beats to send data to **Elasticsearch**, as illustrated in the following diagram:

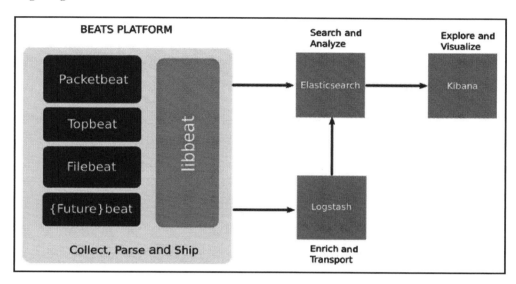

The preceding diagram shows the following Beats:

- **Packetbeat**: This essentially sniffs packets over the network wire for specific protocols such as MySQL and HTTP. It grabs all the fundamental metrics that will be used to monitor the protocol in question. For example, in the case of HTTP, it will get the request, the response, and then wrap it into a document, and index it into Elasticsearch. We'll not use this Beat in the book, as it would require a full book on it, so I encourage you to go on the following website to see what kind of Kibana dashboard you can build on top of it: `http://demo.elastic.co`.

- **Filebeat**: This is meant to securely transport the content of a file from point *A* to point *B*, such as the `tail` command. We'll use this Beat jointly with the new ingest node (`https://www.elastic.co/guide/en/elasticsearch/reference/master/ingest.html`) to push the data from a file directly to Elasticsearch, which will process the data before indexing it. The architecture can then be simplified, as shown in the following diagram:

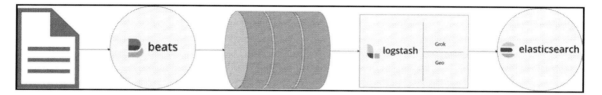

- In the preceding diagram, the data is first shipped by Beats, put into a message broker (we'll come back to this notion later in the book), processed by Logstash, and then indexed by Elasticsearch. The ingest node dramatically simplifies the architecture for the use case:

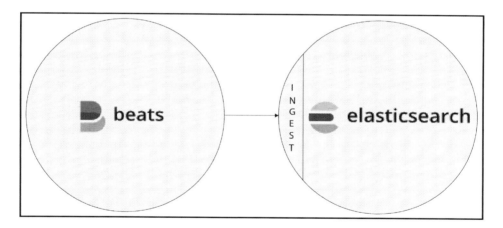

As the preceding diagrams show, the architecture is reduced to two components, with Filebeat and the ingest node. Following this, we'll then be able to visualize the content in Kibana.

- **Topbeat**: This is the first kind of Metricbeat that allows us to ship machines or application execution metrics to Elasticsearch. We'll also use it later on in this book to ship our laptop data and visualize it in Kibana. The good thing here is that this Beat comes with prebuilt templates that only need to be imported in Kibana, as the document generated by the Beat is standard.
- There are a lot of different Beats made by the community that can be used for creating interesting data visualizations. A list of them can be found at `https://www.elastic.co/guide/en/beats/libbeat/current/index.html`.

While these Beats offer some basic filtering features, they don't provide the level of transformation that Logstash can bring.

Logstash

Logstash is a data processor that embraces the centralized data processing paradigm. It allows users to collect, enrich/transform, and transport data to other destinations with the help of more than 200 plugins, as shown in the following diagram:

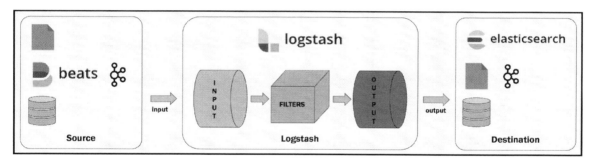

Logstash is capable of collecting data from any source, including Beats, as every Beat comes with out-of-the-box integration for Logstash. The separation of roles is clear here: while Beats is responsible for shipping the data, Logstash allows for processing the data before it is indexed. From a data visualization point of view, Logstash should be used in order to prepare the data; we will see, for example, later in this book, that you could receive IP addresses in logs from which it might be useful to deduce a specific geolocation.

Kibana

Kibana is the core product described in this book; it's where all the user interface actions happen. Most of the visualization technology handles the analytical processing, whereas Kibana is just a web application that renders analytical processing done by Elasticsearch. It doesn't load data from Elasticsearch and process it, but it leverages the power of Elasticsearch to do all the heavy lifting. This essentially allows real-time visualization at scale: as the data grows, the Elasticsearch cluster is scaled relatively, to offer the best latency depending on the SLAs.

Kibana provides visual power to the Elasticsearch aggregations, allowing you to slice through your time series datasets, or segment your data fields, as easy as pie.

Kibana is fitted for time-based visualization, even if your data can come without any timestamp, and brings visualization made for rendering the Elasticsearch aggregation framework. The following screenshot shows an example of a dashboard built in Kibana:

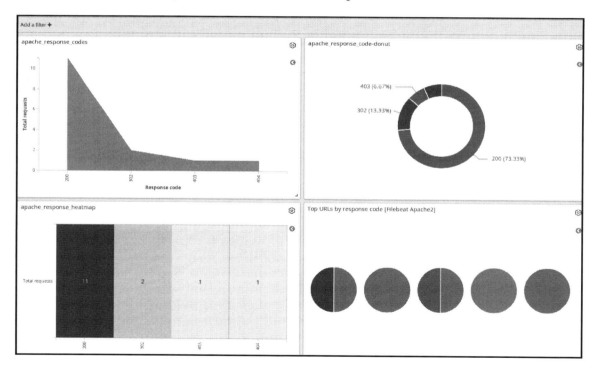

As you can see, a dashboard contains one or more visualizations. We'll dig into them one by one in the context of our use cases. To build a dashboard, the user is brought into a data exploration experience where they can do the following:

- Discover data by digging into the indexed document, as shown in the following screenshot:

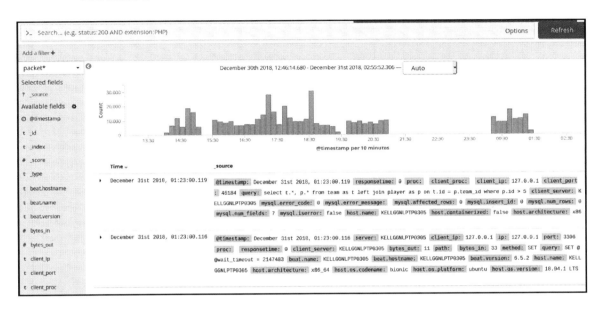

- Build visualizations with the help of a comprehensive palette, based on the question the user has for the data:

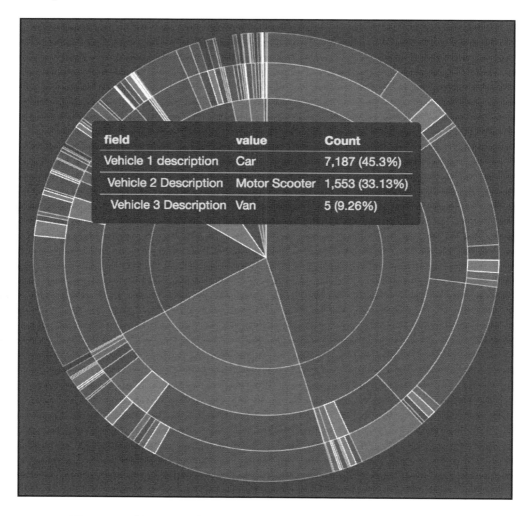

field	value	Count
Vehicle 1 description	Car	7,187 (45.3%)
Vehicle 2 Description	Motor Scooter	1,553 (33.13%)
Vehicle 3 Description	Van	5 (9.26%)

The preceding visualization shows the vehicles involved in an accident in Paris. In this example, the first vehicle was a **Car**, the second was a **Motor Scooter**, and the third was a **Van**. We will dig into the accidentology dataset in the logging use case.

- Build an analytics experience by composing the different visualizations in a dashboard.

X-Pack

Finally, I would like to introduce the concept of X-Pack, which will also be used in the book. While X-Pack is part of the subscription offer, you can download it on the Elastic website and use a trial license to evaluate it.

X-Pack is a set of plugins for Elasticsearch and Kibana that provides the following enterprise features.

Security

Security helps to secure the architecture at the data and access level. On the access side, the Elasticsearch cluster can be integrated with an LDAP, active directory, and PKI to enable role-based access on the cluster. There are additional ways to access it, either by what we call a native realm, which is local to the cluster, or a custom realm, to integrate with other sources of authentication (https://www.elastic.co/guide/en/x-pack/current/security-getting-started.html).

By adding role-based access to the cluster, users will only see data that they are allowed to see at the index level, document level, and field level. From a data visualization point of view, this means, for example, that if a set of users are sharing data within the same index, but the first set is only allowed to see French data and the other set can only see German data, they could both have a Kibana instance pointing to the index, but the underlying permissions configuration, renders the respective country data.

On the data side, the transport layer between Elasticsearch nodes can be encrypted. Transport can also be secured at the Elasticsearch and Kibana level, which means that the Kibana URL can be behind HTTPS. Finally, the security plugin provides IP filtering, but more importantly for data visualization, audit logging that tracks all the access to the cluster and can be easily rendered as a Kibana dashboard.

Monitoring

Monitoring is a Kibana plugin that gives insights into the infrastructure. While this was made primarily for Elasticsearch, Elastic is extending it for other parts of the architecture, such as Kibana or Logstash. That way, users will have a single point of monitoring of all Elastic components and can track, for example, whether Kibana is executing properly, as shown in the following screenshot:

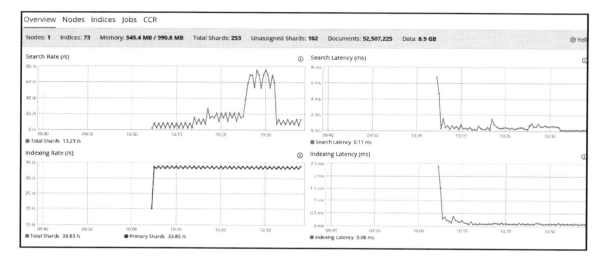

As you can see, users are able to see how many concurrent connections are made on Kibana, as well as deeper metrics such as the event loop delay, which essentially represents the performance of the Kibana instance.

Alerting

If alerting is combined with monitoring data, it then enables proactive monitoring of both your Elastic infrastructure and your data. The alerting framework lets you describe queries to schedule an action in the background to define the following:

- When you want to run the alert; in other words, to schedule the execution of the alert
- What you want to watch by setting a condition that leverages Elasticsearch search, aggregations, and graph APIs
- What you want to do when the watch is triggered, that is, write the result in a file, in an index, send it by email, or send it over HTTP

The watch states are also indexed in Elasticsearch, which allows visualization to see the life cycle of the watch. Typically, you would render a graph that monitors certain metrics and the related triggered watches, as shown in the following diagram:

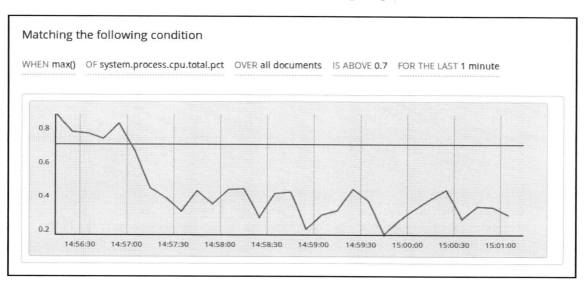

The important aspect of the preceding visualization is that the user can see when the alerts have been triggered and how many of them have been triggered, depending on a threshold. We will use alerting later in this book in a metric analytics use case based on the performance of the CPU.

Reporting

Reporting is a new plugin brought in with the latest version, 2.x, to allow users to export the Kibana dashboard as a PDF. This is one of the most awaited features from Kibana users, and is as simple as clicking on a button, as illustrated in the following screenshot:

The PDF generation is put into a queue and users can follow the export process, and then download the PDF.

Summary

At this point, you should have a clear view of the different components that are required to build up a data-driven architecture. We have also examined how the Elastic Stack fits this need, and have learned how Kibana requires the other components of the stack in order to ship, transform, and store the visualized data. We have also covered how Beats can be quite handy to get data from different servers without putting an extra burden on the servers.

In the next chapter, we'll demonstrate how to get started with Kibana and install all the components you need to see your first dashboard.

Installing and Setting Up Kibana
2

In the last chapter, we discussed data and how we can work with it to get meaningful information. We also covered how the Elastic Stack can help us to analyze the data and to create dashboards with key performance indicators. Now, in this chapter, we will cover the installation process of Elastic Stack 7, where we will look at Elasticsearch, Logstash, Beats, and Kibana.

We will cover the installation process for different types of operating systems in order to make it more useful for a wide range of readers. During the installation of the Elastic Stack, we must maintain the same versions for the entire stack. For example, if we are installing version 7.0 of Elasticsearch, then the same version has to be installed for Beats, Logstash, APM server, and Kibana. This ensures the compatibility between these components. Another thing to bear in mind is the installation order. This has to be done in the order of Elasticsearch, Kibana, Logstash, Beat, and then APM server. In this chapter, we will cover the following topics:

- Installing Elasticsearch
- Installing Kibana
- Installing Logstash
- Installing Beats

Installing Elasticsearch

Elasticsearch is the heart of the Elastic Stack as the storage of data is done in Elasticsearch. There are different ways to install Elasticsearch depending on the operating system that we use. Here, we will cover different ways to install Elasticsearch, such as by using the `.zip` or `.tar.gz` archives, using the `deb` package, using the `rpm` package, using the `msi` package for Windows, or using Docker containers. So, let's start our Elasticsearch installation using the `.zip` or `.tar.gz` archives first.

Elasticsearch installation using the .zip or .tar.gz archives

We can use these packages to install the Elasticsearch software. This comes under the Elastic license, where we can freely use the open source part while commercial features can be used by starting a free 30-day trial duration. On the Elastic downloads page, we can get the latest stable version of Elasticsearch. If we want to install any specific version, then we can do so from the past releases page of the Elastic website. We require Java 8 or later to install Elasticsearch.

Downloading and installing using the .zip archive

The following steps helps us to download and install the Elasticsearch 7.1.0 `.zip` archive file:

1. We can download and install the Elasticsearch 7.1.0 `.zip` archive with the following commands:

```
wget
https://artifacts.elastic.co/downloads/elasticsearch/elasticsearch-
7.1.0-windows-x86_64.zip
wget
https://artifacts.elastic.co/downloads/elasticsearch/elasticsearch-
7.1.0-windows-x86_64.zip.sha512
```

2. After downloading the `.zip` archive, we can match the SHA with the published checksum using the following command:

```
shasum -a 512 -c elasticsearch-7.1.0-windows-x86_64.zip.sha512
```

3. Now, extract the `.zip` archive and navigate inside the directory using the following commands:

```
unzip elasticsearch-7.1.0-windows-x86_64.zip
cd elasticsearch-7.1.0/
```

Downloading and installing using the .tar.gz archive

The following steps helps us to download and install the Elasticsearch 7.1.0 `.tar.gz` archive file:

1. We can download the Elasticsearch 7.1.0 `.tar.gz` archive with the following commands:

```
wget
https://artifacts.elastic.co/downloads/elasticsearch/elasticsearch-
7.1.0-linux-x86_64.tar.gz
wget
https://artifacts.elastic.co/downloads/elasticsearch/elasticsearch-
7.1.0-linux-x86_64.tar.gz.sha512
```

2. After downloading the `.tar.gz` archive, we can compare the SHA with the published checksum using the following command:

```
shasum -a 512 -c elasticsearch-7.1.0-linux-x86_64.tar.gz.sha512
```

3. Now extract the `.tar.gz` archive and navigate inside the directory using the following commands:

```
tar -xzf elasticsearch-7.1.0-linux-x86_64.tar.gz
cd elasticsearch-7.1.0/
```

Running Elasticsearch

After installing the `.zip` or `.tar.gz` archives, we can run Elasticsearch using the following command:

```
./bin/elasticsearch
```

Elasticsearch installation on Windows using the .zip package

On a Windows machine, we can install Elasticsearch using the `.zip` package. In this package, we have the `elasticsearch-service.bat` command through which we can run Elasticsearch as a service. We can get the stable version of Elasticsearch on the download section of the Elastic website. Additionally, we can refer to the past releases page if we want to install any specific version instead of the current version.

Downloading and installing the .zip package

On a Windows machine, we can download the `.zip` package from the download section on the Elastic website. If you want to download any specific version of Elasticsearch, then it can be downloaded from the past releases page on the Elastic website. Here, I am referring to Elasticsearch version 7.1.0. Once the `.zip` package is downloaded, we can unzip it to create the `elasticsearch-7.1.0` folder. Let's say that we have unzipped the `.zip` package in `c:`; we then need to run the following command to navigate inside the folder:

```
cd c:\elasticsearch-7.1.0
```

Running Elasticsearch

Once the Elasticsearch `.zip` package is downloaded and extracted, we can carry out the following steps:

1. Go inside the Elasticsearch home directory and run the following command:

   ```
   .\bin\elasticsearch.bat
   ```

2. ng Elasticsearch, we can test whether it is working properly by running the following command:

   ```
   curl -X GET "localhost:9200/"
   ```

If Elasticsearch is running properly, then we should get the following response:

```
{
  "name" : "ANUGGNLPTP0305",
  "cluster_name" : "elasticsearch",
  "cluster_uuid" : "BIP_9t5fR-SxB72hLM8SwA",
  "version" : {
    "number" : "7.0.0",
    "build_flavor" : "default",
    "build_type" : "deb",
    "build_hash" : "15bb494",
    "build_date" : "2019-02-13T12:30:14.432234Z",
    "build_snapshot" : false,
    "lucene_version" : "8.0.0",
    "minimum_wire_compatibility_version" : "6.7.0",
    "minimum_index_compatibility_version" : "6.0.0"
  },
  "tagline" : "You Know, for Search"
}
```

Installing Elasticsearch as a service

On a Windows machine, we can install Elasticsearch as a service that can run in the background. We can also configure the service to start after every machine boot, which helps us to remove the manual process. We can do this by using the `elasticsearch-service.bat` script in the `bin\` folder of Elasticsearch. Using this script, we can install, configure, start or stop the service, manage, and remove Elasticsearch. We can pass two parameters with this script; the first one is mandatory, whereas the second one is optional.

The first parameter is the command that we want to execute, such as `install` or `remove`, while the second parameter is `SERVICE_ID`, which is useful if we have more than one Elasticsearch service. We will get the following response if we run the `elasticsearch-service.bat` script without any parameter:

```
c:\elasticsearch-7.1.0\bin>elasticsearch-service.bat
Usage: elasticsearch-service.bat install|remove|start|stop|manager
[SERVICE_ID]
```

In the preceding command, we can see the output; it mentions that we need to provide a command such as `install`, `remove`, `start`, and so on, along with the optional `SERVICE_ID` parameter, which is the unique identifier of the running service.

We can pass the following commands to the script:

- `install`: This is if we want to install Elasticsearch as a service
- `remove`: We can use this to remove the Elasticsearch service and also stop the service if it is already running
- `manager`: This command will provide a GUI to manage the service
- `start`: This will start the Elasticsearch service if Elasticsearch is installed
- `stop`: This will stop the Elasticsearch service if the service is started

Elasticsearch installation using the Debian package

We can use the Debian package to install Elasticsearch on Debian, Ubuntu, or other Debian-based systems. We can download the Debian package from the Elastic website or from the `apt` repository. We are free to use the Debian package under the Elastic license. We can get the stable version on the downloads page of the Elastic website. Additionally, if we want to install any specific version, then we can refer to the past releases page on the Elastic website.

Installing Elasticsearch using the apt repository

Before installing Elasticsearch using the `apt` repository, we need to install the `apt-transport-http` package and carry out the following steps:

1. To install this package, we need to run the following command:

```
sudo apt-get install apt-transport-https
```

2. Following this, we can execute the following command to save the repository definition in `/etc/apt/sources.list.d/elastic-7.x.list`:

```
echo "deb https://artifacts.elastic.co/packages/7.x-prerelease/apt stable main" | sudo tee -a /etc/apt/sources.list.d/elastic-7.x.list
```

3. Once the repository definition is saved, we can install the Elasticsearch Debian package using the following command:

```
sudo apt-get update && sudo apt-get install elasticsearch
```

So, in this way, we can install Elasticsearch using the Debian package.

Manually installing using the Debian package

We can download the Debian package of Elasticsearch from the Elastic website. To install it, you can perform the following steps:

1. We can download the `elasticsearch-7.1.0-amd64.deb` Debian package with the following commands:

   ```
   wget
   https://artifacts.elastic.co/downloads/elasticsearch/elasticsearch-
   7.1.0-amd64.deb
   wget
   https://artifacts.elastic.co/downloads/elasticsearch/elasticsearch-
   7.1.0-amd64.deb.sha512
   ```

2. After downloading the Debian package, we can compare the SHA with the published checksum using the following command:

   ```
   shasum -a 512 -c elasticsearch-7.1.0-amd64.deb.sha512
   ```

3. We can install the Debian package using the following command:

   ```
   sudo dpkg -i elasticsearch-7.1.0-amd64.deb
   ```

Using the preceding command, we can install Elasticsearch using the Debian package.

Elasticsearch installation using RPM

Using the RPM package, we can install Elasticsearch on openSUSE, CentOS, or Red Hat-based systems. We can download the RPM package from the Elastic website or from the `apt` repository. We are free to use the RPM package under the Elastic license. We can get the stable version from the downloads page of the Elastic website. Additionally, if we want to install any specific version, then we can refer to the past releases page on the Elastic website.

Installing using the apt repository

First, we need to create a `elasticsearch.repo` file using the following content:

```
[elasticsearch-7.x]
name=Elasticsearch repository for 7.x packages
baseurl=https://artifacts.elastic.co/packages/7.x-prerelease/yum
gpgcheck=1
gpgkey=https://artifacts.elastic.co/GPG-KEY-elasticsearch
```

```
enabled=1
autorefresh=1
type=rpm-md
```

For Red Hat-based distributions, we need to save the file in the `/etc/yum.repos.d/` directory, and, for openSUSE-based distributions, we need to save the file in the `/etc/zypp/repos.d/` directory. Once the file is created and saved, we can install Elasticsearch using the following commands:

- For CentOS and older Red Hat-based distributions, we can use the `yum` command:

```
sudo yum install elasticsearch
```

- For Fedora and new Red Hat-based distributions, we can use the `dnf` command to install Elasticsearch:

```
sudo dnf install elasticsearch
```

- For openSUSE-based distributions, we can install Elasticsearch using `zypper`:

```
sudo zypper install elasticsearch
```

Manually installing using RPM

We can download the RPM package of Elasticsearch from the Elastic website. Then, we can install it using the following steps:

1. We can download the RPM for Elasticsearch v7.1.0 package using the following commands:

```
wget
https://artifacts.elastic.co/downloads/elasticsearch/elasticsearch-
7.1.0-x86_64.rpm
wget
https://artifacts.elastic.co/downloads/elasticsearch/elasticsearch-
7.1.0-x86_64.rpm.sha512
```

2. After downloading the RPM package, we can compare the SHA with the published checksum using the following command:

```
shasum -a 512 -c elasticsearch-7.1.0-x86_64.rpm.sha512
```

3. We can install the RPM package using the following command:

```
sudo rpm --install elasticsearch-7.1.0-x86_64.rpm
```

Using the preceding command, we can install Elasticsearch using the RPM package.

Running Elasticsearch

We can run Elasticsearch in two ways, as follows:

- Running Elasticsearch with SysV
- Running Elasticsearch with systemd

Running Elasticsearch with SysV

Using the `chkconfig` command, we can configure Elasticsearch to automatically start on each reboot:

```
sudo chkconfig --add elasticsearch
```

If we want to start Elasticsearch, we need to run the following command:

```
sudo -i service elasticsearch start
```

To stop Elasticsearch, we need to run the following command:

```
sudo -i service elasticsearch stop
```

Running Elasticsearch with systemd

We need to run the following command if we want to start Elasticsearch automatically after each reboot:

```
sudo /bin/systemctl daemon-reload
sudo /bin/systemctl enable elasticsearch.service
```

To start Elasticsearch, we need to run the following command:

```
sudo systemctl start elasticsearch.service
```

To stop Elasticsearch, we need to run the following command:

```
sudo systemctl stop elasticsearch.service
```

The preceding commands do not provide any update on STDOUT telling us whether the command was successful or not. We can see these updates in the Elasticsearch log file, which can be found in the /var/log/elasticsearch/ directory.

Checking whether Elasticsearch is running

After running Elasticsearch, we can test whether it is working properly by running the following command:

```
curl -X GET "localhost:9200/"
```

If Elasticsearch is running properly, then we should get the following response:

```
{
  "name" : "ANUGGNLPTP0305",
  "cluster_name" : "elasticsearch",
  "cluster_uuid" : "BIP_9t5fR-SxB72hLM8SwA",
  "version" : {
    "number" : "7.0.0-beta1",
    "build_flavor" : "default",
    "build_type" : "deb",
    "build_hash" : "15bb494",
    "build_date" : "2019-02-13T12:30:14.432234Z",
    "build_snapshot" : false,
    "lucene_version" : "8.0.0",
    "minimum_wire_compatibility_version" : "6.7.0",
    "minimum_index_compatibility_version" : "6.0.0-beta1"
  },
  "tagline" : "You Know, for Search"
}
```

So far, we have installed Elasticsearch, started the Elasticsearch service, and tested the service by running it using `curl`. Now we will cover how to install Kibana and then run it.

Installing Kibana

Kibana is the UI for the Elastic Stack and is primarily used for data analysis and visualization. There are different ways to install Elasticsearch depending on the operating system we use. Here, we will cover different ways to install Elasticsearch, such as by using the `.zip` or `.tar.gz` archives, using the `deb` package, using the `rpm` package, using the `msi` package for Windows, or using Docker containers. So, let's start the Elasticsearch installation using the `.zip` or `.tar.gz` archives first.

Kibana installation using the .zip or .tar.gz archives

On Linux, we can use the `tar.gz` package to install Kibana, while the `.zip` package can be used to install Kibana on Windows. Installing using the `tar.gz` or `.zip` package is the easiest way to do this, as we just need to download the package and install it.

Downloading and installing using the .tar.gz archive

We can use the `.tar.gz` Kibana package for installation on Linux systems. For installing Kibana, this is the easiest way; by carrying out the following steps:

1. We can install Kibana by downloading the Linux archive using the following command:

   ```
   wget
   https://artifacts.elastic.co/downloads/kibana/kibana-7.1.0-linux-x8
   6_64.tar.gz
   ```

2. Then, we can verify the file by validating the SHA created with the published SHA, using the following command:

   ```
   shasum -a 512 kibana-7.1.0-linux-x86_64.tar.gz
   ```

3. Following this, we can extract the `.tar.gz` package using the following command:

   ```
   tar -xzf kibana-7.1.0-linux-x86_64.tar.gz
   ```

4. Now, you can navigate inside the extracted directory using the following command:

   ```
   cd kibana-7.1.0-linux-x86_64/
   ```

Running Kibana

To run Kibana, we need to run the following command:

```
./bin/kibana
```

Using the preceding command, we can run Kibana; we just need to make sure that the command is being executed from the Kibana home directory, that is, the extracted Kibana directory.

Downloading and installing using the .zip archive

We can install Kibana on a Windows machine using the `.zip` package of Kibana. We can get the latest stable version of Kibana from the download section of the Elastic website. If you want to download any specific version of Kibana, then you can do so from the past releases page on the Elastic website. Here, I am referring to version 7.1.0 of Kibana. Once the `.zip` package is downloaded, we can unzip it to create the `kibana-7.1.0` folder. Let's say that we have unzipped the `.zip` package in `c:`; we now need to run the following command to navigate inside the folder:

```
CD c:\kibana-7.1.0-windows-x86_64
```

Running Kibana

Once the Kibana `.zip` package is downloaded and extracted, we can go inside the Kibana home directory and run the following command:

```
.\bin\kibana.bat
```

After running the preceding command, we can see the logs in STDOUT as Kibana, by default, runs in the foreground. We can stop Kibana by pressing *Ctrl + C*.

Kibana installation using the Debian package

We can use the Debian package to install Kibana on Debian, Ubuntu, or other Debian-based systems. We can download the Debian package from the Elastic website or from the `apt` repository. We are free to use the Debian package under the Elastic license. We can get the stable version from the downloads page of the Elastic website. Additionally, if we want to install any specific version, then we can refer to the past releases page on the Elastic website.

Installing using the apt repository

Before installing Kibana using the `apt` repository, we need to install the `apt-transport-http` package as follows:

1. To install this package, we need to run the following command:

   ```
   sudo apt-get install apt-transport-https
   ```

2. Following this, we can execute the following command to save the repository definition in `/etc/apt/sources.list.d/elastic-7.x.list`:

   ```
   echo "deb https://artifacts.elastic.co/packages/7.x-prerelease/apt stable main" | sudo tee -a /etc/apt/sources.list.d/elastic-7.x.list
   ```

3. Once the repository definition is saved, we can install the Kibana Debian package using the following command:

   ```
   sudo apt-get update && sudo apt-get install kibana
   ```

So, in this way, we can install Kibana using the Debian package.

Manually installing Kibana using the Debian package

We can download the Debian package of Kibana from the Elastic website and install it using the following steps:

1. We can download the `kibana-7.1.0-amd64.deb` Debian package using the following commands:

   ```
   wget https://artifacts.elastic.co/downloads/kibana/kibana-7.1.0-amd64.deb
   ```

2. After downloading the Debian package, we can compare the SHA with the published checksum using the following command:

   ```
   shasum -a 512 kibana-7.1.0-amd64.deb
   ```

3. We can install the Debian package using the following command:

   ```
   sudo dpkg -i kibana-7.1.0-amd64.deb
   ```

Using the preceding command, we can install Kibana using the Debian package.

Running Kibana

We can run Kibana in two ways, as follows:

- Running Kibana with SysV
- Running Kibana with systemd

Running Kibana with SysV

Using the `chkconfig` command, we can configure Kibana to automatically start on each reboot:

```
sudo update-rc.d kibana defaults 95 10
```

If we want to start Kibana, we need to run the following command:

```
sudo -i service kibana start
```

To stop Kibana, we need to run the following command:

```
sudo -i service kibana stop
```

Running Kibana with systemd

We need to run the following command if we want to start Kibana automatically after each reboot:

```
sudo /bin/systemctl daemon-reload
sudo /bin/systemctl enable kibana.service
```

To start Kibana, we need to run the following command:

```
sudo systemctl start kibana.service
```

To stop Kibana, we need to run the following command:

```
sudo systemctl stop kibana.service
```

The preceding commands do not provide any update on STDOUT telling us whether the command was successful or not. We can see these updates on the Kibana log file that can be found in the `/var/log/kibana/` directory.

Kibana installation using RPM

Using the RPM package, we can install Kibana on openSUSE, CentOS, or Red Hat-based systems. We can download the RPM package from the Elastic website or from the `apt` repository. We are free to use the RPM package under the Elastic license. We can get the stable version from the downloads page of the Elastic website. Additionally, if we want to install any specific version, then we can refer to the past releases page on the Elastic website.

Installing using the apt repository

First, we need to create a `kibana.repo` file using the following content:

```
[kibana-7.x]
name=Kibana repository for 7.x packages
baseurl=https://artifacts.elastic.co/packages/7.x-prerelease/yum
gpgcheck=1
gpgkey=https://artifacts.elastic.co/GPG-KEY-elasticsearch
enabled=1
autorefresh=1
type=rpm-md
```

For Red Hat-based distributions, we need to save the file in the `/etc/yum.repos.d/` directory, and, for openSUSE-based distributions, we need to save the file in the `/etc/zypp/repos.d/` directory. Once the file is created and saved, we can install Elasticsearch using the following commands:

- For CentOS and older Red Hat-based distributions, we can use the `yum` command:

  ```
  sudo yum install kibana
  ```

- For Fedora and new Red Hat-based distributions, we can use the `dnf` command to install Kibana:

  ```
  sudo dnf install kibana
  ```

- For openSUSE-based distributions, we can install Kibana using `zypper`:

  ```
  sudo zypper install kibana
  ```

Manually installing using RPM

We can download the RPM package of Kibana from the Elastic website and can install it using the following steps:

1. We can download the RPM for Kibana v7.1.0 package using the following commands:

```
wget https://artifacts.elastic.co/downloads/kibana/kibana-7.1.0-
x86_64.rpm
```

2. After downloading the RPM package, we can compare the SHA with the published checksum using the following command:

```
shasum -a 512 kibana-7.1.0-x86_64.rpm
```

3. We can install the RPM package using the following command:

```
sudo rpm --install kibana-7.1.0-x86_64.rpm
```

Using the preceding command, we can install Kibana using the RPM package.

Running Kibana

We can run Kibana in two ways, as follows:

- Running Kibana with SysV
- Running Kibana with systemd

Running Kibana with SysV

Using the `chkconfig` command, we can configure Kibana to automatically start on each reboot:

```
sudo chkconfig --add kibana
```

If we want to start Kibana, then we need to run the following command:

```
sudo -i service kibana start
```

To stop Kibana, we need to run the following command:

```
sudo -i service kibana stop
```

Running Kibana with systemd

We need to run the following command if we want to start Kibana automatically after each reboot:

```
sudo /bin/systemctl daemon-reload
sudo /bin/systemctl enable kibana.service
```

To start Kibana, we need to run the following command:

```
sudo systemctl start kibana.service
```

To stop Kibana, we need to run the following command:

```
sudo systemctl stop kibana.service
```

The preceding commands do not provide any update in STDOUT telling us whether the command was successful or not. We can see these updates on the Elasticsearch log file that can be found in the `/var/log/kibana/` directory.

Installing Logstash

Logstash is an open source real-time pipelining and data collection engine. Logstash requires Java 8 to be installed on the machine, so you will need to verify whether Java 8 is installed. Additionally, Logstash does not support Java 9, so you need to stick with Java 8 for now. For checking the installed version of Java, you need to run the following command:

```
java -version
```

Once Java version 8 is verified, you can proceed with the Logstash installation.

Installing Logstash using the downloaded binary

We can download the Logstash binary installation file from the Elastic website at `https://www.elastic.co/downloads/logstash`. After downloading the file, we need to unpack it. We can freely use these packages under the Elastic license.

Installing Logstash from the package repositories

We can install Logstash using repositories based on the distribution, such as apt or yum.

Installing Logstash using the apt package

First of all, we need to install the public signing key after downloading it using the following command:

```
wget -qO - https://artifacts.elastic.co/GPG-KEY-elasticsearch | sudo apt-key add -
```

On Debian, we need to install the apt-transport-https package before installing Logstash:

```
sudo apt-get install apt-transport-https
```

Next, we need to save the repository definition in /etc/apt/sources.list.d/elastic-7.x-prerelease.list using the following command:

```
echo "deb https://artifacts.elastic.co/packages/7.x-prerelease/apt stable main" | sudo tee -a /etc/apt/sources.list.d/elastic-7.x-prerelease.list
```

Now we can update the repository and then install Logstash using the following command:

```
sudo apt-get update && sudo apt-get install logstash
```

In this way, we can install Logstash using the apt package.

Installing Logstash using the yum package

For the yum package, we need to first install the public signing key after downloading it using the following command:

```
rpm --import https://artifacts.elastic.co/GPG-KEY-elasticsearch
```

We need to create a file with the .repo suffix, for example, logstash.repo in the /etc/yum.repos.d/ directory; then, add the following content to the file:

```
[logstash-7.x]
name=Elastic repository for 7.x packages
baseurl=https://artifacts.elastic.co/packages/7.x-prerelease/yum
gpgcheck=1
gpgkey=https://artifacts.elastic.co/GPG-KEY-elasticsearch
```

```
enabled=1
autorefresh=1
type=rpm-md
```

Once the file is created, our repository is ready, and we can install Logstash using the following command:

```
sudo yum install logstash
```

In this way, we can install Logstash using `yum`.

Running Logstash as a service

After installing Logstash, we will need to start it manually. This is because, after installation, Logstash is not started automatically by default. There are different ways to start and stop Logstash based on the system, that is, whether it uses SysV, systemd, or upstart.

Running Logstash using systemd

The systemd unit file for Logstash is located in `/etc/systemd/system` for `deb` and `rpm`. After installing Logstash, we can start it using the following command:

```
sudo systemctl start logstash.service
```

To stop Logstash, we can run the following command:

```
sudo systemctl stop logstash.service
```

In this way, we can start and stop the Logstash service on systemd-based systems.

Running Logstash using upstart

To start Logstash on systems that use upstart, we can run the following command:

```
sudo initctl start logstash
```

To stop Logstash, we can run the following command:

```
sudo initctl stop logstash
```

In this way, we can start and stop the Logstash service on upstart-based systems.

Running Logstash using SysV

To start Logstash on systems that use SysV, we can run the following command:

```
sudo /etc/init.d/logstash start
```

To stop Logstash, we can run the following command:

```
sudo /etc/init.d/logstash stop
```

In this way, we can start and stop the Logstash service on SysV-based systems. Next, we will demonstrate how to install Beats.

Installing Beats

Beats are lightweight, single-purpose data shippers that can be installed on servers to send data to Logstash or Elasticsearch. There are different Beats for different purposes, such as Filebeat, Packetbeat, Winlogbeat, Metricbeat, Heartbeat, and more. We will cover the installation of some different types of Beats in this section.

Installing Filebeat

Depending on the system, we have different options for installing Filebeat.

deb

For installing Filebeat on Debian systems, we need to run the following commands:

```
curl -L -O
https://artifacts.elastic.co/downloads/beats/filebeat/filebeat-7.0.0-beta1-
amd64.deb
sudo dpkg -i filebeat-7.0.0-beta1-amd64.deb
```

rpm

For installing Filebeat using the RPM package, we need to run the following commands:

```
curl -L -O
https://artifacts.elastic.co/downloads/beats/filebeat/filebeat-7.0.0-beta1-
x86_64.rpm
sudo rpm -vi filebeat-7.0.0-beta1-x86_64.rpm
```

macOS

To install Filebeat on a macOS system, we need to run the following commands:

```
curl -L -O
https://artifacts.elastic.co/downloads/beats/filebeat/filebeat-7.0.0-beta1-
darwin-x86_64.tar.gz
tar xzvf filebeat-7.0.0-beta1-darwin-x86_64.tar.gz
```

Linux

To install Filebeat on a Linux machine, we need to run the following commands:

```
curl -L -O
https://artifacts.elastic.co/downloads/beats/filebeat/filebeat-7.0.0-beta1-
linux-x86_64.tar.gz
tar xzvf filebeat-7.0.0-beta1-linux-x86_64.tar.gz
```

win

To install Filebeat on a Windows machine, we need to perform the following steps:

1. Download the Windows ZIP package from the downloads page of the Elastic website
2. Extract the ZIP file from `C:\Program Files`
3. Rename the extracted folder to `Filebeat` from `filebeat-<version>-windows`
4. Run the following command to install `Filebeat` from the PowerShell prompt, which we need to open as the administrator:

```
PS > cd 'C:\Program Files\Filebeat'
PS C:\Program Files\Filebeat> .\install-service-filebeat.ps1
```

Installing Metricbeat

Depending on the system, we have different options for installing Metricbeat.

deb

To install Metricbeat on Debian systems, we need to run the following commands:

```
curl -L -O
https://artifacts.elastic.co/downloads/beats/metricbeat/metricbeat-7.0.0-
beta1-amd64.deb
sudo dpkg -i metricbeat-7.0.0-beta1-amd64.deb
```

rpm

To install Metricbeat using the RPM package, we need to run the following commands:

```
curl -L -O
https://artifacts.elastic.co/downloads/beats/metricbeat/metricbeat-7.0.0-
beta1-x86_64.rpm
sudo rpm -vi metricbeat-7.0.0-beta1-x86_64.rpm
```

macOS

To install Metricbeat on a macOS system, we need to run the following commands:

```
curl -L -O
https://artifacts.elastic.co/downloads/beats/metricbeat/metricbeat-7.0.0-
beta1-darwin-x86_64.tar.gz
tar xzvf metricbeat-7.0.0-beta1-darwin-x86_64.tar.gz
```

Linux

To install Metricbeat on a Linux machine, we need to run the following commands:

```
curl -L -O
https://artifacts.elastic.co/downloads/beats/metricbeat/metricbeat-7.0.0-
beta1-linux-x86_64.tar.gz
tar xzvf metricbeat-7.0.0-beta1-linux-x86_64.tar.gz
```

win

To install Metricbeat on a Windows machine, we need to perform the following steps:

1. Download the Windows ZIP package from the downloads page of the Elastic website
2. Extract the ZIP file from `C:\Program Files`

3. Rename the extracted folder to `Metricbeat` from `metricbeat-<version>-windows`

4. Run the following command to install `Metricbeat` from the PowerShell prompt, which we need to open as the administrator:

```
PS > cd 'C:\Program Files\Metricbeat'
PS C:\Program Files\Metricbeat> .\install-service-metricbeat.ps1
```

Installing Packetbeat

Depending on the system, we have different options for installing Packetbeat.

deb

To install Packetbeat on Debian systems, we need to run the following commands:

```
sudo apt-get install libpcap0.8
curl -L -O
https://artifacts.elastic.co/downloads/beats/packetbeat/packetbeat-7.0.0-beta1-amd64.deb
sudo dpkg -i packetbeat-7.0.0-beta1-amd64.deb
```

rpm

To install Packetbeat using the RPM package, we need to run the following commands:

```
sudo yum install libpcap
curl -L -O
https://artifacts.elastic.co/downloads/beats/packetbeat/packetbeat-7.0.0-beta1-x86_64.rpm
sudo rpm -vi packetbeat-7.0.0-beta1-x86_64.rpm
```

macOS

To install Packetbeat on a macOS system, we need to run the following commands:

```
curl -L -O
https://artifacts.elastic.co/downloads/beats/packetbeat/packetbeat-7.0.0-beta1-darwin-x86_64.tar.gz
tar xzvf packetbeat-7.0.0-beta1-darwin-x86_64.tar.gz
```

Linux

To install Packetbeat on a Linux machine, we need to run the following commands:

```
curl -L -O
https://artifacts.elastic.co/downloads/beats/packetbeat/packetbeat-7.0.0-
beta1-linux-x86_64.tar.gz
tar xzvf packetbeat-7.0.0-beta1-linux-x86_64.tar.gz
```

win

To install Packetbeat on a Windows machine, we need to perform the following steps:

1. Download the Windows ZIP package from the downloads page of the Elastic website
2. Extract the ZIP file from `C:\Program Files`
3. Rename the extracted folder to Packetbeat from `packetbeat-<version>-windows`
4. Run the following command to install `Packetbeat` from the PowerShell prompt, which we need to open as the administrator:

   ```
   PS > cd 'C:\Program Files\Packetbeat'
   PS C:\Program Files\Packetbeat> .\install-service-packetbeat.ps1
   ```

Installing Heartbeat

Heartbeat is a lightweight data shipper that is used to monitor services. Depending on the system, we have different options for installing Heartbeat.

deb

To install Heartbeat on a Debian system, we need to run the following commands:

```
curl -L -O
https://artifacts.elastic.co/downloads/beats/heartbeat/heartbeat-7.0.0-
beta1-amd64.deb
sudo dpkg -i heartbeat-7.0.0-beta1-amd64.deb
```

rpm

To install Heartbeat using the RPM package, we need to run the following commands:

```
curl -L -O
https://artifacts.elastic.co/downloads/beats/heartbeat/heartbeat-7.0.0-
beta1-x86_64.rpm
sudo rpm -vi heartbeat-7.0.0-beta1-x86_64.rpm
```

macOS

To install Heartbeat on a macOS system, we need to run the following commands:

```
curl -L -O
https://artifacts.elastic.co/downloads/beats/heartbeat/heartbeat-7.0.0-
beta1-darwin-x86_64.tar.gz
tar xzvf heartbeat-7.0.0-beta1-darwin-x86_64.tar.gz
```

Linux

To install Heartbeat on a Linux machine, we need to run the following commands:

```
curl -L -O
https://artifacts.elastic.co/downloads/beats/heartbeat/heartbeat-7.0.0-
beta1-linux-x86_64.tar.gz
tar xzvf heartbeat-7.0.0-beta1-linux-x86_64.tar.gz
```

win

To install Heartbeat on a Windows machine, we need to perform the following steps:

1. Download the Windows ZIP package from the downloads page of the Elastic website
2. Extract the ZIP file from `C:\Program Files`
3. Rename the extracted folder to Heartbeat from `heartbeat-<version>-windows`
4. Run the following command to install `Heartbeat` from the PowerShell prompt, which we need to open as the administrator:

   ```
   PS > cd 'C:\Program Files\Heartbeat'
   PS C:\Program Files\Heartbeat> .\install-service-heartbeat.ps1
   ```

Installing Winlogbeat

To install Winlogbeat on a Windows machine, we need to perform the following steps:

1. Download the Winlogbeat Windows ZIP package from the downloads page of the Elastic website
2. Extract the ZIP file from `C:\Program Files`
3. Rename the extracted folder to `Winlogbeat` from `winlogbeat-<version>-windows`
4. Run the following command to install `Winlogbeat` from the PowerShell prompt, which we need to open as the administrator:

```
PS C:\Users\Administrator> cd 'C:\Program Files\Winlogbeat'
PS C:\Program Files\Winlogbeat> .\install-service-winlogbeat.ps1
```

In this way, we can install Winlogbeat on a Windows machine.

Summary

In this chapter, we covered the installation of the Elastic Stack. We started by installing Elasticsearch on different types of machines, and then we covered the installation of Kibana on different types of machines. Note that you should follow the correct sequence in order to install the complete Elastic Stack on your machine. Following this, we also looked at the installation of Logstash on different types of machines. Finally, we covered the installation of different Beats, including Filebeat Metricbeat, Packetbeat, Heartbeat, and Winlogbeat.

In the next chapter, we will cover business analytics with Kibana. We will learn how to analyze the data that is pushed into Elasticsearch by creating an index pattern.

Section 2: Exploring the Data 2

In this section, we will cover data input using Beats and Logstash, and learn how to analyze data using Discover. We will also learn how to visualize data using Kibana Visualize, and how to create Dashboards in Kibana.

The following chapters will be covered in this section:

- Chapter 3, *Business Analytics with Kibana*
- Chapter 4, *Data Visualization Using Kibana*

Business Analytics with Kibana

3

At this point, we should have the Elastic Stack installed and be able to start creating dashboards and visualizations. In this chapter, we will focus on the logging analytics use case, where we will explore how to analyze Apache log data and then we will cover data ingestion using CSV files, the **Relational Database Management System (RDBMS)** database using MySQL, and NoSQL using MongoDB. We will use Beats for ingesting the Apache logs and we will use Logstash for ingesting MySQL and MongoDB data.

In this chapter, we will cover the following topics:

- Understanding logs
- Data modeling
- Importing data
- Beats
- Configuring Filebeat to import data
- Logstash
- Reading CSV data using Logstash
- Reading MongoDB data using Logstash
- Reading MySQL data using Logstash
- Creating an index pattern

Understanding logs

I would like to start this chapter by discussing logs, as they are a very important part of any system. By using log information, we can access the details of a system relatively easily. But what is a log? Well, a **log** is an event that contains a timestamp and a description of the event itself. It is appended to a journal or log file sequentially, where all of the lines of the logs are ordered based on the timestamp. As an example, here is an Apache server log:

```
127.0.0.1 - - [02/Apr/2019:10:15:22 +0530] "POST /blog/admin.php HTTP/1.1"
302 326 "http://localhost/blog/admin.php" "Mozilla/5.0 (X11; Ubuntu; Linux
x86_64; rv:66.0) Gecko/20100101 Firefox/66.0"
```

Looking at the preceding code, we can guess the meaning of certain information, such as an IP address (`127.0.0.1`), a timestamp (`02/Apr/2019:10:15:22 +0530`), an HTTP verb (`POST`), and the queried resource (`/blog/admin.php`). All of this information is essential for different purposes, such as analyzing the traffic on your server, detecting suspicious behavior, or leveraging data in order to enhance user experience on your website.

Before visualization applications came in as the de facto solution for analyzing logs, IT operations teams generally implemented massive GREP commands on this data in order to extract the gist of it. However, this is no longer welcomed in environments where data is growing to reach a scale where it is not humanly feasible to cope by only using GREPs.

 GREP is a command-line utility that we can use to search a plaintext dataset. Essentially, it returns the matching lines for a provided regular expression.

Kibana provides the ability to simplify log management, first, through the visualization of the obvious data, but also by discovering magic moments, in other words, unexpected data.

Data modeling

Like every product, the Elastic Stack comes with best practices for data modeling. Kibana renders the data that comes as a result of aggregation in Elasticsearch. Elasticsearch does aggregations on data in the same index. The index contains documents that contain fields. As a consequence, the more consistent the documents are, the more scope you will have for aggregating data. By consistency in documents, we mean as many fields as possible to describe an event, or, in other words, an entity. This is what we call an entity-centric document.

In the case of our example, here is how the raw data is structured:

```
10000101,HY190020,03/18/2015 10:09:00 PM,036XX S WOLCOTT
AVE,1811,NARCOTICS,POSS: CANNABIS 30GMS OR
LESS,STREET,true,false,0912,009,11,59,18,1164279,1880656,2015,02/10/2018
03:50:01 PM,41.828138428,-87.672782106,"(41.828138428, -87.672782106)"
```

This is a comma-separated log line that describes crime incidents and records in Chicago; the dataset is publicly available on the U.S. government website (`https://catalog.data.gov/dataset/crimes-2001-to-present-398a4`). It contains `ID`, `Case Number`, `Date`, `Block`, `IUCR`, `Primary Type`, `Description`, `Location Description`, `Arrest`, `Domestic`, `Beat`, `District`, `Ward`, `Community Area`, `FBI Code`, `X Coordinate`, `Y Coordinate`, `Year`, `Updated On`, `Latitude`, `Longitude`, and `Location`. If we transform this line into a proper JSON document, which is what Elasticsearch expects, here is what it looks like:

```
{
    "ID": "10000101",
    "Community Area": "59",
    "FBI Code": "18",
    "District": "009",
    "Domestic": "false",
    "Case Number": "HY190020",
    "Block": "036XX S WOLCOTT AVE",
    "@timestamp": "2018-10-13T11:33:45.622Z",
    "Description": "POSS: CANNABIS 30GMS OR LESS",
    "Beat": "0912",
    "Location Description": "STREET",
    "Latitude": "41.828138428",
    "Ward": "11",
    "Date": "03/18/2015 10:09:00 PM",
    "Year": "2015",
    "Updated On": "02/10/2018 03:50:01 PM",
    "X Coordinate": "1164279",
    "Y Coordinate": "1880656",
    "Longitude": "-87.672782106",
    "Arrest": "true",
    "IUCR": "1811",
    "Primary Type": "NARCOTICS",
    "host": "ANUGGNLPTP0305",
    "Location": "(41.828138428, -87.672782106)"
}
```

The preceding commands are easier to read, and this is preferred in Elasticsearch in order to have different possibilities in terms of aggregations. This will allow us to obtain certain information from the data, such as the case number of any document and the type of crime. To import the CSV data, we will use Logstash, where we will read the CSV values, map them with the field names, and push them into Elasticsearch.

In this way, we can transform different types of data; for example, we can transform unstructured data, such as log data, into structured data using Logstash and send it to the centralized Elasticsearch cluster. From this Elasticsearch cluster, the data can be visualized using Kibana. The core functionality of the Elastic Stack is to ingest different types of data in Elasticsearch using Logstash or Beats. Then, using Kibana, we can do the magic. In Kibana, we have different options to play around with the data and, by using those tools, we can present the data in a meaningful way to get the details out of it.

In any working application, we have logs; however, for the most part, they are scattered. This means that, if we want to search for something, we need to dig into the logs in order to find it. This approach is known as a reactive approach, where we dig into the logs in order to fetch some information. But it is better to configure data through some tool so that it can tell us the story of past, present, and future data in a very simple way, for example, what is happening, how it is happening, and what is causing it to happen. These are very common questions, and we can get the answers from different sources. Consider a system in which we can get this information in a combined way, and where all factors are throwing the data and providing us with a uniform view of the data, to search through, in order to gain a complete insight of an issue. The Elastic Stack can help us to build a system where we can do all of this.

Importing data

There are different ways in which we can import data into Elasticsearch, such as using Beats, which can be installed on any server and can send data, or using Logstash, which can fetch data from different sources and send it to a central Elasticsearch server or cluster. Essentially, we have two primary options in the Elastic Stack for importing data: Beats and Logstash. Here, we will cover both of them in detail and we will discover ways to configure them to fetch data.

Beats

Beats are essentially lightweight, single-purpose data shippers that can be installed on servers to read the data and send it directly to the Elasticsearch server or through Logstash. There are different types of Beats based on the type of jobs they perform:

- **Filebeat**: Using Filebeat, we can read file data, such as system log file data, application log file data, or any other file type that is there on the server.
- **Metricbeat**: Using Metricbeat, we can fetch system metrics from the server on which Metricbeat is installed, such as CPU usage, memory usage, disk utilization, and more.
- **Packetbeat**: To read the server packet data, we can use Packetbeat; it keeps on reading the network packets and forwards it to Elasticsearch.
- **Heartbeat**: Using Heartbeat, we can keep on monitoring the services if they are up and running. We can configure API endpoints to check whether the API is working, or we can listen to a specific port. Essentially, by using Heartbeat, we can monitor different services, URLs, ports, and more.
- **Functionbeat**: Using Functionbeat, we can monitor the data from our cloud services. It can be deployed as a function on the **Function-as-a-Service** (**FaaS**) platform of the cloud provider. Once it is deployed, it starts collecting the data and ships it to Elasticsearch.
- **Winlogbeat**: Using Winlogbeat, we can monitor the Windows-based infrastructure as it live-streams Windows event logs, which can be sent directly to Elasticsearch or through Logstash.

The following diagram shows a view where we are fetching data using different Beats and sending it to Elasticsearch:

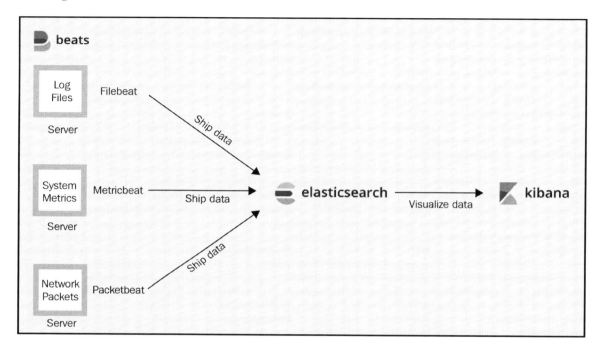

In the preceding diagram, we have **Filebeat** reading the **Log Files**, **Metricbeat** reading the **System Metrics**, and **Packetbeat** reading the **Network Packets**. After reading the data, they ship it to the Elasticsearch server from where **Kibana** is reading the data to visualize it.

Configuring Filebeat to import data we need to enable the following command in the input section of the filebeat.yml file

Using Filebeat, we can read any file data whether it is an application log file, system log file, or any other file data. It is quite handy, as we just need to install it on a server and configure the locations from where we want to read the file data.

In the previous chapter, we covered how to install Filebeat; so, after the installation, we now need to configure Filebeat so that it can start reading the data from the desired files from a location. Input and harvesters are the two main components of Filebeat that work together for reading different files. A harvester is used to open, close, and read individual files so its count will with the total number of files we are going to read. Input, essentially, manages harvesters and finds all of the locations from where it needs to read the data.

First, we need to edit the `filebeat.yml` file for configuring Filebeat. To edit the file, we can open it using the following command:

```
sudo vim /etc/filebeat/filebeat.yml
```

Using the preceding command, we can open the configuration file of Filebeat. Note that the location of this file can vary on the basis of the operating system that you are using. Additionally, there are different sections of the configuration, such as Filebeat input, where we can define the location with the filename to read:

```
#============================ Filebeat inputs ============================

filebeat.inputs:

# Each - is an input. Most options can be set at the input level, so
# you can use different inputs for various configurations.
# Below are the input specific configurations.

- type: log

  # Change to true to enable this input configuration.
  enabled: false

  # Paths that should be crawled and fetched. Glob based paths.
  paths:
    - /var/log/*.log
```

In the preceding example, we can configure the location to read the file. We mentioned `/var/log/*.log` so that Filebeat can read logs from the `/var/log/` location and the wildcard (*) will ensure that it will read all of the files that have the `.log` extension.

Following this, we can configure the `output` section and send the log data that Filebeat harvests to an Elasticsearch server.

The following snippet shows the `output` section of the configuration file:

```
#================================ Outputs ================================
```

```
# Configure what output to use when sending the data collected by the beat.

#------------------------- Elasticsearch output -------------------------
----
output.elasticsearch:
  # Array of hosts to connect to.
  hosts: ["localhost:9200"]

  # Optional protocol and basic auth credentials.
  #protocol: "https"
  #username: "elastic"
  #password: "changeme"

#-------------------------- Logstash output --------------------------
----
#output.logstash:
  # The Logstash hosts
  #hosts: ["localhost:5044"]

  # Optional SSL. By default is off.
  # List of root certificates for HTTPS server verifications
  #ssl.certificate_authorities: ["/etc/pki/root/ca.pem"]

  # Certificate for SSL client authentication
  #ssl.certificate: "/etc/pki/client/cert.pem"

  # Client Certificate Key
  #ssl.key: "/etc/pki/client/cert.key"
```

In the `output` section, we have two options: `Elasticsearch output` and `Logstash output`. This means that we can send our data directly to Elasticsearch or we can send through Logstash. If we are using the Elastic Cloud service, then we can just provide `cloud.id` in the Elastic Cloud section of the configuration file:

```
cloud.id:
"staging:dXMtZWFzdC0xLmF3cy5mb3VuZC5pbyRjZWM2ZjI2MWE3NGJmMjRjZTMzYmI4ODExYj
g0Aeq0ZeRjNmMyY1E2ZDA0MjI0OWFmMGNjN2Q3YTllOTYyNTc0Mw=="
```

We can use a sample Kibana dashboard for Filebeat; for that, we need to set the Kibana endpoint, as follows:

```
setup.kibana:
  host: "kibanahost:5601"
```

We can use Filebeat modules to work on common log formats such as nginx, Apache, and MySQL. By enabling the module, we can enable Filebeat to take care of all possible data for that module. Let's say that we want to monitor Apache using Filebeat; so, when we enable Apache using the Filebeat module, it will read the access file and error file of Apache and will combine the data from which we can easily know what is happening in a time frame.

We can list, enable, or disable the Filebeat module. Additionally, we have a separate configuration file for each module that we can modify as per our need.

Reading log files using Filebeat

Let's say that we want to read all of the log files data from the /var/log location. To do so, we need to enable the following command in the input section of the filebeat.yml file:

```
paths:
  - /var/log/*.log
```

The preceding pattern will ensure that we can read all of the files that end with the .log extension in the /var/log/ directory. After configuring the input block, we need to configure the output section to send the log data either to Logstash or to Elasticsearch. Here, we are configuring it to send logs directly to the Elasticsearch server and, for that, we need to configure the Elasticsearch output section using the following expression:

```
output.elasticsearch:
  # Array of hosts to connect to.
  hosts: ["localhost:9200"]
```

Once we have modified the filebeat.yml file, we can start the Filebeat service to start fetching the log data. To verify whether everything is working properly, we can list the indices in Elasticsearch and can check whether we have an index that starts with filebeat- using the following command:

```
curl -XGET "http://localhost:9200/_cat/indices"
```

If we get the Filebeat index in the Elasticsearch indices listing, then our configuration is working fine; otherwise, we should verify whether the service is working properly or, alternatively, we can check the Filebeat log file to try and understand the issue. Filebeat stores the log file in the following format:

```
{
  "_index": "filebeat-7.0.0-2019.04.12-000001",
  "_type": "_doc",
  "_id": "PXReV2kBk7_BaA5ItrH1",
  "_version": 1,
  "_score": null,
```

```
      "_source": {
        "agent": {
          "hostname": "ANUGGNLPTP0305",
          "id": "83179236-86ac-4116-bdea-64b770a8bd49",
          "type": "filebeat",
          "ephemeral_id": "8bdda5da-8902-4dc7-a7a3-39546c7092ec",
          "version": "7.0.0"
        },
        "log": {
          "file": {
            "path": "/var/log/apache2/access.log.1"
          },
          "offset": 2468
        },
        "source": {
          "address": "127.0.0.1",
          "ip": "127.0.0.1"
        },
        "fileset": {
          "name": "access"
        },
        "url": {
          "original":
"/test/admin.php?server=125.16.240.217&amp;username=liveuser&amp;db=msehat&
amp;script=kill"
        },
        "input": {
          "type": "log"
        },
        "apache": {
          "access": {}
        },
        "@timestamp": "2019-02-14T07:12:27.000Z",
        "ecs": {
          "version": "1.0.0-beta2"
        },
        "service": {
          "type": "apache"
        },
        "host": {
          "hostname": "ANUGGNLPTP0305",
          "os": {
            "kernel": "4.15.0-45-generic",
            "codename": "bionic",
            "name": "Ubuntu",
            "family": "debian",
            "version": "18.04.2 LTS (Bionic Beaver)",
            "platform": "ubuntu"
```

```
        },
        "containerized": false,
        "name": "ANUGGNLPTP0305",
        "id": "3981136c89ec40e496c3b850831321fe",
        "architecture": "x86_64"
      },
      "http": {
        "request": {
          "referrer":
"http://localhost/test/admin.php?server=125.16.240.217&amp;username=liveuse
r&amp;db=msehat&amp;select=families",
          "method": "POST"
        },
        "response": {
          "status_code": 200,
          "body": {
            "bytes": 209
          }
        },
        "version": "1.1"
      },
      "user_agent": {
        "original": "Mozilla/5.0 (X11; Ubuntu; Linux x86_64; rv:64.0)
Gecko/20100101 Firefox/64.0",
        "os": {
          "name": "Ubuntu"
        },
        "name": "Firefox",
        "device": {
          "name": "Other"
        },
        "version": "64.0"
      }
    },
    "fields": {
      "suricata.eve.timestamp": [
        "2019-02-14T07:12:27.000Z"
      ],
      "@timestamp": [
        "2019-02-14T07:12:27.000Z"
      ],
      "event.created": [
        "2019-03-07T08:56:56.215Z"
      ]
    }
  }
}
```

In this way, by using Filebeat, we can fetch the log file data in Elasticsearch. It also converts the unstructured log data into structured data. Similarly, we can configure Metricbeat or Packetbeat to start fetching data. We configure Metricbeat when we want to get system metrics, such as the CPU usage and memory; whereas, Packetbeat is used to read packet details on a server.

We have explored how to install and configure Filebeat to read log data. Now, we will discuss how to configure Logstash to read different types of data such as CSV files, MongoDB, or MySQL.

Logstash

Logstash is a server-side data processing pipeline that we can use to ingest data from different sources, such as logs, CSV files, databases, Kafka, or Elasticsearch, through the `input` plugin of Logstash. After ingesting the data, we can transform it using the `filter` plugin of Logstash. Then, we can send data to different sources, such as Elasticsearch, or files, using the `output` plugin. By using the `input`, `filter`, and `output` plugins, we can read data from different sources, transform them, and send them to different sources. Additionally, Logstash is an open source data processing pipeline, so we can freely use it.

Here, we are going to demonstrate how we can import data from CSV, MySQL, and MongoDB to Elasticsearch.

Reading CSV data using Logstash

Here, we will use the **Popular Baby Names** dataset as an example, which has been taken from the Data.gov website (`https://catalog.data.gov/dataset/most-popular-baby-names-by-sex-and-mothers-ethnic-group-new-york-city-8c742`). This is open data, so we can freely download and use it. To begin, the format of the data contains `Year of Birth`, `Gender`, `Ethnicity`, `Child's First Name`, `Count`, and `Rank`. The following example shows a snippet of the actual CSV data:

Year of Birth	Gender	Ethnicity	Child's First Name
Count	Rank		
2016	FEMALE	ASIAN AND PACIFIC ISLANDER	Olivia
172	1		
2016	FEMALE	ASIAN AND PACIFIC ISLANDER	Chloe
112	2		
2016	FEMALE	ASIAN AND PACIFIC ISLANDER	Sophia
104	3		
2016	FEMALE	ASIAN AND PACIFIC ISLANDER	Emily
99	4		

```
2016            FEMALE    ASIAN AND PACIFIC ISLANDER    Emma
99      4
```

The preceding dataset displays only the initial five lines of the actual CSV data, which I have downloaded from the Data.gov website for **Popular Baby Names**, but the actual file (`Popular_Baby_Names.csv`) contains 11,345 records. Now, we will configure Logstash to read this CSV file to fetch the data and send it to Elasticsearch. The Logstash configuration file is saved inside the `Downloads` directory from where we will read the CSV data in Logstash.

Now, as we know, in order to read any type of data, we need to configure the `input` plugin of Logstash.

To transform any input data, we need to configure the `filter` plugin, and, to output the data, we need to configure the `output` plugin as follows:

1. Create the Logstash configuration file, `popular_baby.conf`, to read the CSV data, as follows:

```
input {
    file {
        path => "/home/user/Downloads/Popular_Baby_Names.csv"
        start_position => beginning
    }
}
filter {
    csv {
        columns => [
                "Year of Birth",
                "Gender",
                "Ethnicity",
                "Child's First Name",
                "Count",
                "Rank"
        ]
        separator => ","
        }
}
output {
    stdout
    {
        codec => rubydebug
    }
     elasticsearch {
        action => "index"
        hosts => ["127.0.0.1:9200"]
```

```
            index => "Popular_Baby_Names"
    }
}
```

In the preceding `filter` option, we have provided the column names to map as, in this case, we can provide any name to map with the field. If we want to autodetect the field names from CSV, then we can write the following expression in `filter`:

```
filter {
  csv {
    autodetect_column_names => true
  }
}
```

2. Once the configuration file is created, we can execute the file to fetch the CSV data and push it to Elasticsearch.

3. To execute the Logstash configuration file, we need to move inside the Logstash home directory and then run the following command:

bin/logstash -f /etc/logstash/conf.d/popular_baby.conf

4. After executing the preceding command, we will get a success message, as follows:

[Api Webserver] agent – Successfully started Logstash API endpoint {:port=>9600}

After this, Logstash will start fetching the CSV data line by line and will map the column names given in the `filter` plugin in the CSV module. We have also configured the standard output in order to see the output on the Terminal using `rubydebug codec` to format the `output` data. By doing so, we can see the following output on the screen:

```
{
            "@timestamp" => 2019-04-13T12:58:22.673Z,
                "Gender" => "MALE",
         "Year of Birth" => "2011",
              "@version" => "1",
             "Ethnicity" => "WHITE NON HISPANIC",
    "Child's First Name" => "PARKER",
                 "Count" => "16",
                  "Rank" => "91",
                  "path" =>
"/home/user/Downloads/Popular_Baby_Names.csv",
                  "host" => "ANUGGNLPTP0305",
```

```
                "message" => "2011,MALE,WHITE NON
HISPANIC,PARKER,16,91"
        }
```

This ensures that we are getting the proper mapping of our CSV data and that the same formatted JSON will also be pushed to Elasticsearch.

5. To verify whether the index has been created, we can execute the following command:

   curl −XGET "http://localhost:9200/_cat/indices"

   This will list all of the available indices in Elasticsearch from which we can search the popular-baby-names index.

6. Once we have found the index, we can view the documents in the index using the following command:

   curl −XGET "http://localhost:9200/popular-baby-names/_search"

   This will list the documents inside the popular-baby-names index; take a look at the following example that shows a single document inside index:

```
    {
            "_index" : "popular-baby-names",
            "_type" : "_doc",
            "_id" : "RjXGFmoB75utKkMR3eUI",
            "_score" : 1.0,
            "_source" : {
              "@timestamp" : "2019-04-13T12:58:10.693Z",
              "Gender" : "FEMALE",
              "Year of Birth" : "2014",
              "@version" : "1",
              "Ethnicity" : "WHITE NON HISPANIC",
              "Child's First Name" : "Dylan",
              "Count" : "33",
              "Rank" : "63",
              "path" : "/home/user/Downloads/Popular_Baby_Names.csv",
              "host" : "ANUGGNLPTP0305",
              "message" : "2014,FEMALE,WHITE NON HISPANIC,Dylan,33,63"
        }
    }
```

In this way, we can import the data from the CSV files to Elasticsearch. Now, the question that arises is why we need to do this at all, as we can open the data in any spreadsheet application and apply a filter or search to get the desired results.

It is useful to mention that spreadsheet applications have certain limitations, and we cannot do a lot of things in the spreadsheet that can easily be done in Elastic Stack. Once the data is in Elasticsearch, we can apply aggregations, create different types of visualizations in Kibana, and apply machine learning.

Reading MongoDB data using Logstash

For reading MongoDB data through Logstash, we need the `logstash-input-mongodb` plugin. This does not come by default with Logstash, so we need to install it as follows:

1. Use the following command from the home Logstash directory:

    ```
    bin/logstash-plugin install logstash-input-mongodb
    ```

    To run the preceding command, we need to switch to the root user; otherwise, it will give privilege error. Once the command is successfully executed, we will get the following response:

    ```
    Validating logstash-input-mongodb
    Installing logstash-input-mongodb
    Installation successful
    ```

2. Once the `logstash-input-mongodb` plugin is installed successfully, we can create the Logstash configuration file to read the MongoDB collection data into Elasticsearch. However, before we do that, we need to check whether the MongoDB server is running, that we can connect to it, and that it has the collection we want to fetch using Logstash.

3. After verifying this, we can create the Logstash configuration file, `blogs.conf`, to read the MongoDB data:

    ```
    input {
     uri => 'mongodb://username:password@mongodb_host:27017'
     placeholder_db_dir => '/opt/logstash-mongodb/'
     placeholder_db_name => 'logstash_sqlite.db'
     collection => 'blogs'
     batch_size => 5000
    }
    filter {

    }
    output {
     stdout {
     codec => rubydebug
     }
     elasticsearch {
    ```

```
action => "index"
index => "blogs_data"
hosts => ["localhost:9200"]
  }
}
```

In the preceding expression, in the input section, we are providing `uri` for the MongoDB server. From here, we are passing a connection string with the username, the password, and the MongoDB host with the port. `placeholder_db_dir` defines the location for the placeholder database. `placeholder_db_name` defines the name of the SQLite database. `collection` tells Logstash which MongoDB collection to pick from the database.

4. Finally, `batch_size` is used to restrict the number of records in a batch. Note that we are not going to filter anything, and that is why this section is left blank.

5. Under `output` again, we are going to set `stdout` to print the output on the Terminal and `elasticsearch` to push the data into Elasticsearch. Once the data is pushed into Elasticsearch, we can view it in the same way as we did the CSV data.

Reading MySQL data using Logstash

We can pull data from the MySQL database to Elasticsearch through Logstash using the `input` JDBC plugin. Using this plugin, we can fetch data from different data sources that support the JDBC connection. So, next, we will try to fetch the data from multiple tables by joining them through a query.

Here, we will pull data in an incremental way by marking a tracking column that can hold the last value. Whenever new data is available in the MySQL table, it will start from the last value to fetch the incremental value and set the tracking column again with the most recent value.

Let's take an example of a blog database where I am storing different blog data. You can take any database with any sort of value to play around with. Now, I have data in three different tables that I want to join using the following query:

```
"SELECT blg.*, concat(au.first_name, ' ',au.last_name) as name,au.email as
email, cc.category_name, cc.category_image  FROM `blog_blogs` as blg left
join auth_user as au on au.id = blg.author_id left join category_category
as cc on cc.id = blg.category_id order by blg.create_date"
```

In the preceding query, I am fetching data from the `blog_blogs`, `auth_user` and `category_category` tables. From the main blog table, I am fetching all of the blogs; from the user table, I am fetching the user's first name, last name, email, and more; and from the category table, I am fetching the category name and category image.

So far, I know what data I want to fetch from my database. I don't want to pull all of the data from there because it will increase the data size and the resource utilization. Another thing that I want to do is to make this process incremental so that I don't need to pull the data again and again whenever there is any new data in the database. So, we need to consider how we can achieve this using the `input` JDBC plugin.

Here, our query is very straightforward as it picks all of the records at once. So, we need to modify the query with something like the following:

```
"SELECT blg.*, concat(au.first_name, ' ',au.last_name) as name,au.email as
email, cc.category_name, cc.category_image  FROM `blog_blogs` as blg left
join auth_user as au on au.id = blg.author_id left join category_category
as cc on cc.id = blg.category_id where blg.id > 10 order by
blg.create_date"
```

Here, we have a column ID that can be checked using the last inserted ID to ensure that this query can always fetch the most recent records from the database. So, we have fixed this issue, but now we need to figure out how to hold the last fetched ID, so that whenever the query runs after a break, it can continue from the last fetched ID. To fix this issue, we have the option of `tracking_column`, where we can set the field to start tracking the changes. Logstash stores the value of this field in a `.logstash_jdbc_last_run` file in the home directory.

So, let's now start writing the Logstash configuration file, `blog_data.conf`, where we need to put all of these plugins:

```
# file: blog_data.conf
input {
    jdbc {
        # path of jdbc driver library
        jdbc_driver_library => "/usr/share/logstash/mysql-connector-
java-5.1.23-bin.jar"
        jdbc_driver_class => "com.mysql.jdbc.Driver"
        # mysql jdbc connection string to the database
        jdbc_connection_string => "jdbc:mysql://db-
host:3306/db_name?zeroDateTimeBehavior=convertToNull"
        # username and password of MySQL database
        jdbc_user => "username"
        jdbc_password => "password"
        # schedule to run the query
```

```
        schedule => "* * * * *"
        # The query with a join of three tables to fetch blog details
        statement => "SELECT blg.*, concat(au.first_name, ' ',au.last_name)
as name,au.email as email, cc.category_name, cc.category_image  FROM
`blog_blogs` as blg left join auth_user as au on au.id = blg.author_id left
join category_category as cc on cc.id = blg.category_id where blg.id >
:sql_last_value order by blg.create_date"
        use_column_value => true
        # tracking column to hold the value through Logstash
        tracking_column => id
        tracking_column_type => "numeric"
    }
}
output {
    elasticsearch {
        hosts => "http://127.0.0.1:9200"
        index => "blog_data"
        document_type => "blogs"
        }
}
```

In the preceding Logstash configuration file, we have the JDBC module in the `input` plugin to create the connection, execute the query, hold the value of the tracking column, and run a scheduler. In the `input` section, we can configure the scheduler by using the schedule parameter. It is quite similar to the `cron` Linux entry with five stars (*):

```
"* * * * * " => if we want to run every second
"35 4 * * *" => runs as 4:35 AM
"15 23 * * *" => runs at 11:15 PM
```

In the `output` plugin section, we are pushing the fetched data to Elasticsearch. In this way, we can execute any query to fetch the data and push that to the Elasticsearch server. After writing the `blog_data.conf` file, we can execute the configuration file using the following command:

```
/usr/share/logstash/bin/logstash -f /etc/logstash/conf.d/blog.conf
```

If we are already running an instance of the Logstash configuration, then we can execute the other ones by adding the `--path.data` parameter in the query. For this parameter, we can set any path and, for each new pipeline, we can change this value to a new file location:

```
/usr/share/logstash/bin/logstash -f /etc/logstash/conf.d/blog.conf --
path.data=/tmp/bq
```

In this way, we can create the Logstash configuration to fetch the MySQL data and push it to Elasticsearch.

Creating an index pattern

By using any of the preceding ways, we can push the data into Elasticsearch. However, in order to analyze it or visualize it in Kibana, we need to create an index pattern in Kibana. So, let's create an index pattern for the `popular-baby-names` index of Elasticsearch that we created by accessing the CSV file using Logstash. To create the index pattern in Kibana, we need to perform the following steps:

1. Click on the **Management** link in the left-hand menu and it will open the **Management** page. On the left, you can see the **Elasticsearch** and **Kibana** options. The following screenshot shows the **Management** options, with the **Index Patterns** link under **Kibana**:

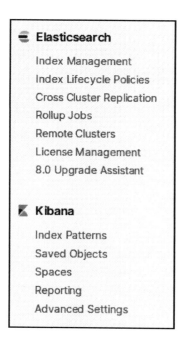

2. Under the **Kibana** listing, we need to click on the **Index Patterns** option, which will open a page with the **Create index pattern** button. Click on the button to open the following page:

3. Now, we need to add the Elasticsearch index name to the **Index pattern** textbox. If successful, we will get a success message, as shown in the following screenshot:

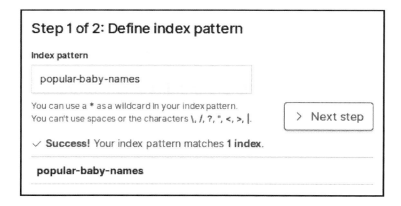

4. Now, we need to click on the **Next step** button; this opens a screen from which you can select **Time Filter field name**. The following screenshot shows the time filter selection page:

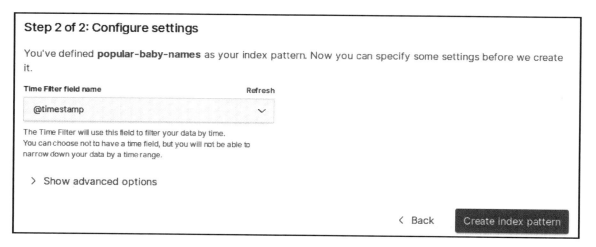

Step 2 of 2: Configure settings

You've defined **popular-baby-names** as your index pattern. Now you can specify some settings before we create it.

Time Filter field name   Refresh

@timestamp   ∨

The Time Filter will use this field to filter your data by time.
You can choose not to have a time field, but you will not be able to
narrow down your data by a time range.

> Show advanced options

‹ Back   Create index pattern

5. After selecting **Time Filter field name**, we need to click on the **Create index pattern** button to create the **Index pattern** using the Elasticsearch index. This will open the following screen:

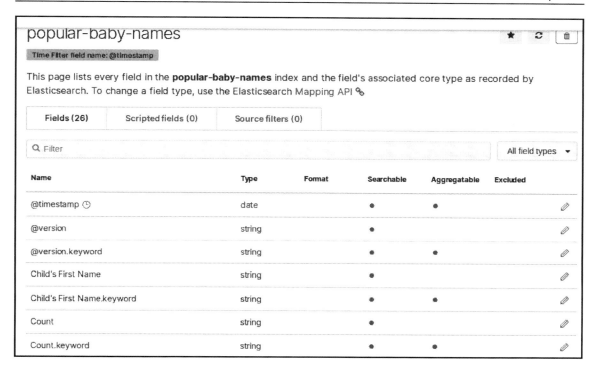

6. In the preceding screenshot, we can see that the index pattern is created with a listing of field names and the option to edit each of them. Using the top three options, we can make this index pattern the default, refresh it, or delete it.

In this way, we can create an index pattern for any of the Elasticsearch indices. For any Beat index, we can use a wildcard (*) to pattern match all of the possible index names, as it creates a daily index using the date. Once the index pattern is created, we can use the Elasticsearch index data in Kibana for analysis and visualization.

Summary

In this chapter, we covered different aspects of business analytics with Kibana. We started with an introduction to data modeling and then we learned about data imports with Beats and Logstash. In Beats, we covered different types of Beats such as Filebeat, Metricbeat, Packetbeat, Heartbeat, Functionbeat, and Winlogbeat.

Following this, we learned how to configure Filebeat to import data from different log files and provided the practical approach to reading log files using Filebeat. Next, we looked at Logstash, including a basic introduction of Logstash and some different use cases. We learned how to read CSV data using Logstash, how to fetch MongoDB collection data into Elasticsearch using Logstash, and how to fetch MySQL data and send it to Elasticsearch using Logstash. Finally, we created an index pattern in Kibana in order to make Elasticsearch data available in Kibana.

In the next chapter, we will cover data visualization and dashboard creation.

Visualizing Data Using Kibana

In this chapter, we are going to cover data visualization, and we will learn how to create dashboards using data. This is an important chapter of this book, as we have covered the introduction, installation, and data ingestion of Kibana, but now we are going to visually represent data in different forms of Kibana visualizations, and then we will consolidate them to create a meaningful dashboard. We will learn how to create a pie chart, bar chart, area chart, tag cloud, data table, map representation of data, heat map, and more. So, basically, we can monitor many things using the Kibana visualization, and here we will see an example of system metrics, which we can monitor using **Metricbeat** data. In the same way, we can monitor the network packets, file data, or application data.

In this chapter, we are going to cover the following topics:

- Creating visualizations in Kibana
- Creating an area, line, and bar chart
- Modifying the visualizations, ordering them, and embedding them
- Creating the dashboard by adding different visualizations
- Embedding the visualization and dashboard on a web page
- Generating the reports from dashboards

Creating visualizations in Kibana

So, if we talk about the Kibana visualization, we have many options to choose from, and it all depends on the type of requirement; for example, we can use a pie chart if we want to display the composition of data such as the composition of each item in the complete set. A bar chart or a line chart can be used to show data distribution, where we just want to understand how data is distributed.

We can also create stacked bar charts, where we can check the distribution of different items and also the individual components of the item. Using the Kibana tag cloud, we can create a visualization with different words, which we can easily filter on the dashboard. This way, based on our requirement, we can create different types of visualizations.

The following screenshot shows different visualization options in Kibana:

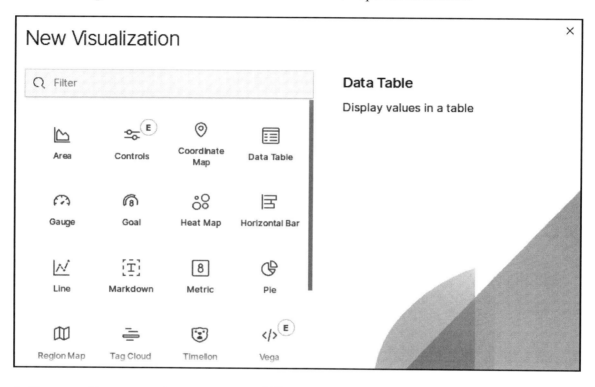

In the preceding screenshot, we can see different types of visualizations, such as **Area**, **Controls**, **Heat Map**, **Pie**, **Line**, **Data Table**, **Metric**, and more. So, now let's jump into the Kibana **Visualize** option and see how we can create different visualizations.

Identifying the data to visualize

For data visualization, we will pick the data from the Metricbeat index pattern, as I am running Metricbeat, and it is pushing the metrics data into Elasticsearch. We have identified that Metricbeat data can be used to create the area type visualization. Now, before we create the visualization, we have to identify the fields that we are going to use for the visualization. But, before that, we should know what all the different fields are that we are getting under Metricbeat data. So, for that, we need to check the Metricbeat index pattern under Kibana **Discover**.

The following link has a screenshot that shows the Metricbeat data under Kibana **Discover**, where we can play around with different fields and can identify the field names, which we should use to create the visualization: `https://github.com/PacktPublishing/Learning-Kibana-7-Second-Edition/tree/master/Images`

The screenshot shows the Metricbeat data after creating the `metricbeat*` index pattern. Here, we can search, filter, and select specific fields to explore the data.

> We have covered index pattern creation in `Chapter 3`, *Business Analytics with Kibana*.

So, using Metricbeat data, we will now create different visualizations.

Creating an area chart, a line chart, and a bar chart

So, the first visualization that we are going to create is an area chart; it is basically a type of chart where we show a different color or texture for the area between the axis and the line. Let's say we want to know the count of different Metricset names that are coming through Metricbeat.

To create an area chart, we need to do the following:

1. Click on the **Visualize** option in the left-hand menu, which will open the **Visualize** page.
2. From this page, click on the plus icon to create a new visualization.
3. From the **New Visualization** popup, click on one of the **Area**, **Line**, or **Bar** option to create the type of chart you want. I am selecting the area chart here.
4. This will open the page to select the data option, where we have two options: **From a New Search, Select Index** and **Or, From a Saved Search**. Using the first option, we can pick the new index, while using the second option, we can pick any saved search, which we can create using Kibana's **Discover** page. The following screenshot shows the data selection page:

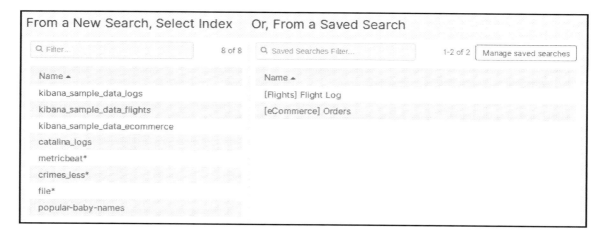

5. In the preceding page, we will select the index pattern, **metricbeat***, as we are going to create the area chart using Metricbeat data. So, for that, we need to click on the **metricbeat*** link under **From a New Search, Select Index**. This will open the following screen:

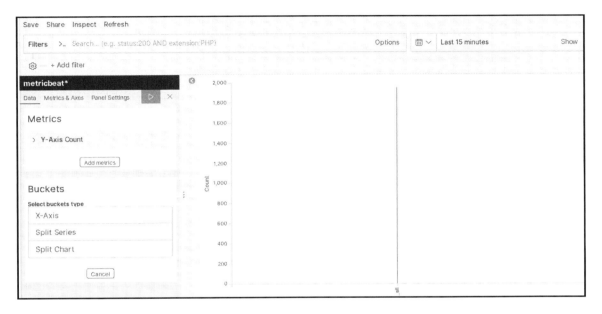

6. We need to set the **Count** for the **Aggregation** dropdown for the **Y-Axis** under **Metrics**, as we want to see the count of different Metricset names. We can set the **Custom Label** as per the **Y-Axis**, so, here, we are changing it to **Total count**.

7. Under **Buckets**, we need to choose **Terms** for the **Aggregation** dropdown under the **X-Axis**.

8. Then, select the **metricset.name** option under the **Field** dropdown.

9. Under the **Order By** dropdown, we can select the field name that we want to sort. So, here, we are selecting the metric: **Total count**, which we have used for the **Y-Axis**.

10. Under the **Order** dropdown, we can select **Descending** or **Ascending**.

11. Now we can select the size that we want to show in the chart. We are changing it to **10** to show the top 10 Metricset names.

12. Now click on the **Apply changes** button to show the visualization. It will create a visualization, as shown in the following screenshot:

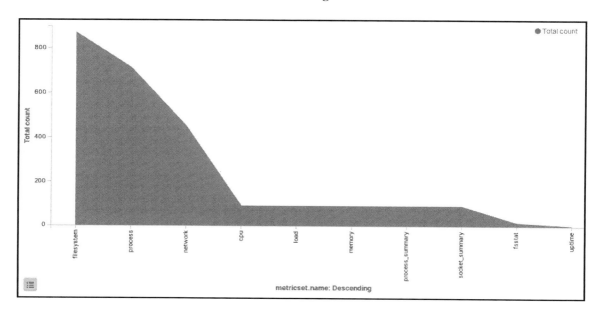

13. After creating the area chart, we can change the chart type into a line chart or a bar chart by clicking on the **Metrics & Axes** panel and then selecting the **Chart Type** dropdown under the **Metrics** option. The following screenshot shows the same chart, which has been changed into a bar chart:

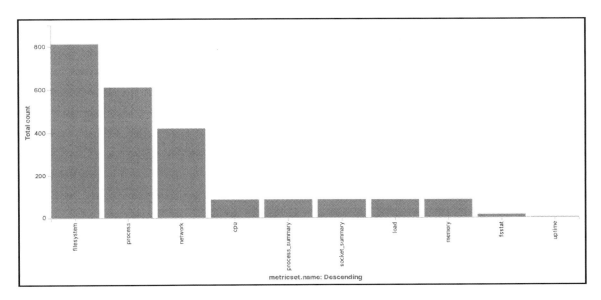

This way, we can create the area chart, line chart, or bar chart to show the count of different Metricset names.

Once the visualization is created, we can save it by clicking on the **Save** link in the top-left of the page; this will open a pop-up menu, where we need to provide the **Title** and then click on the **Confirm Save** button.

Creating a pie chart

Using pie charts, we can display the composition of each item in the complete set. If we have a total of 100 items, then what is the proportion of each type of item among the 100 items? Here, we will take the same example to create the visualization; so, to create the pie chart, we have to do the following:

1. Click on the **Pie** option by selecting the visualization type page. This will open the data selection page.
2. Select the **metricbeat*** index pattern, as we want to see the name of different Metricsets in the chart. This will open the new **pie chart** visualization screen.
3. Under the **Y-Axis**, select **Count** under **Aggregation**, and change the **Custom Label** to **Total requests**.
4. Click on **Split Slices** under **Buckets**, choose **Terms** under **Aggregation**, and select **metricset.name** under **Field** option.
5. Set **Order By** and provide the **Size** as per your requirement, as this may vary.
6. Under **Custom Label**, provide a relevant label such as `Metricset name`.
7. Now click on the **Apply Changes** button to apply these changes and create the pie chart visualization, as shown in the following screenshot:

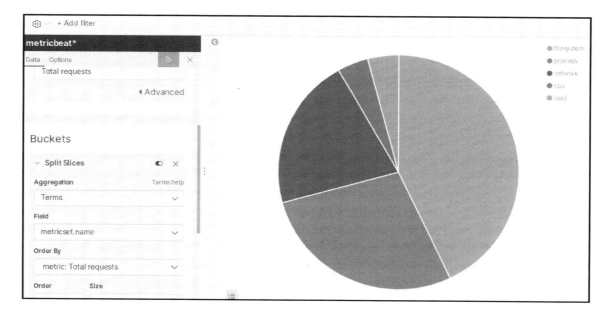

This way, we can create a pie chart, and, here, we can use any field to create the chart.

We can change the pie chart to a donut chart by clicking on the **Options** link to open the options panel and then selecting the **Donut** option. It will convert the pie chart into a donut chart, as shown in the following screenshot:

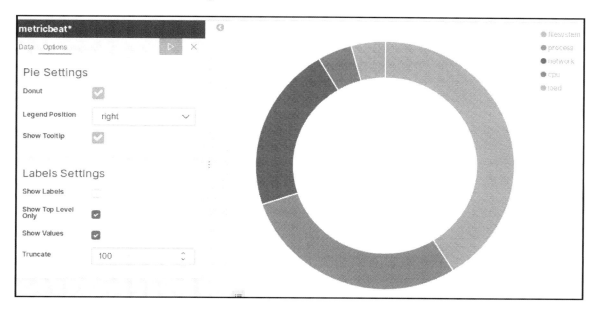

Using the **Options** panel, we can configure different things such as **Pie Settings**, under which we can convert the pie chart into a donut chart, change the legend position, and enable or disable the tooltip. Then, we have **Labels Settings**, using which we can show or hide the labels, show values, truncate values, and more.

Creating the heatmap

In heatmaps, colors are the main differentiators between different sets of data values. Using this type of visualization, it is easy to differentiate between the variations. To create a heatmap in Kibana, we have to do the following:

1. On the **Select visualization type** page, click on the **Heat Map** option. This will open the index selection page.
2. Select the **metricbeat*** index, as we want to create a heat map using the name **Metricset**.
3. This will open the new **Heat Map** visualization screen.
4. Under **Y-Axis**, select **Count** under **Aggregation** and change the **Custom Label** to **Total records**.
5. In **X-Axis**, under **Buckets**, select **Terms** under **Aggregation** and select **metricset.name** under **Field** option.
6. Provide the **Size** as per your requirement, as this may vary.
7. Under **Custom Label**, provide a relevant label such as `Name of metricset`.
8. Now click on the **Apply Changes** button to apply these changes and create the heatmap chart visualization. This will open the following screen:

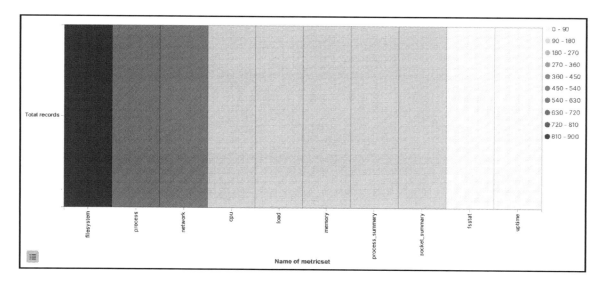

In the preceding screenshot, we can see the different colors for the different types of Metricsets; the **filesystem** Metricset is in red, with a range of **810 - 900**, while the **process** Metricset is in orange, with a range of **720 - 810**. This way, we can easily differentiate among different ranges with different colors, and this is quite easy to understand. We can create the heatmap in Kibana using any field value.

Creating the data table

Using a visualization data table type, we can represent data in a tabular form. The graphical chart is a good way to visualize the data, but the data table helps us to see the actual data with the important columns so that we can see the actual field values. When we add data tables along with the graphical charts, they both work in a synchronized way to provide a complete insight into the data. To create the data table in Kibana, we need to do the following:

1. On the **Select visualization type** page, click on the **Data Table** option. This will open the index selection page.
2. Select the **metricbeat*** index pattern, as we want to create a data table using the Metricbeat Metricset data types. This will open the **New Visualization** screen.
3. Under **Metrics**, select the **Count** option under **Aggregation**, and change the **Custom Label** to **Total requests**.
4. Click on **Add metrics**, as we want to add one more metric. If required, you can add more metrics to your data table.
5. Now add the columns by selecting the **Terms** option under **Aggregation** and the **metricset.name** option under the **Field** dropdown. Set the **Order** and **Size** dropdowns as per the requirement. You can also change the **Custom Label** as per the chosen column.
6. We can add more columns by clicking on the **Split Rows** link and then by repeating the same process, which we did to add the **metricset.name** column.

7. So, I have added the **event.dataset** field here as a column in the data table. The following screenshot shows the data table of the Metricset name and the event dataset:

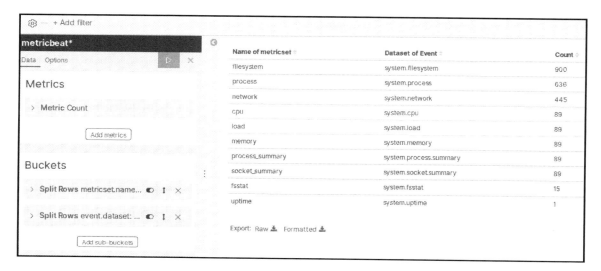

This way, we can create a data table using the index fields so that we can add them to the dashboard to provide a tabular view of the data along with a graphical representation of the data.

Creating the metric visualization

Using the metric visualization, we can display the count or numbers in any field of the index. We can show the count, sum, and average for a different possible set of values for a field in the index. Let's see an example where we want to show the count of different Metricset types using their names. In this scenario, we can easily use the metric type of visualization. To add this, we need to do the following:

1. On the **Select visualization type** page, click on the **Metric** option. This will open the index selection page.
2. Select the **metricbeat*** index pattern, as we want to create a metric display using the Metricbeat Metricset data types. This will open the **New Visualization** screen.
3. Under **Metrics**, select the **Count** option in **Aggregation**, and change the **Custom Label** to **Total requests**.

4. Click on **Add metrics**, as we want to add one more metric. If required, you can add more metrics to your visualization.
5. Click on the **Split Group** link under **Buckets** to add columns.
6. Choose **Terms** under **Aggregation** and select **metricset.name** or any field you want to display.
7. Now click on the **Apply Changes** button to apply these changes that will create the metric type visualization, as shown on the following screenshot:

In the preceding screenshot, we can see the **Total requests** for each value of the **metricset.name** field, and, in the same way, we can create the metric view for any field in the index. In a dashboard, we need different types of visualizations to make it more effective and meaningful.

Creating the tag cloud

The **tag cloud** is also very good and intuitive visualization option for any dashboard. We can configure it to show keywords using any field of the index, which can be clicked and filtered using the tag cloud visualization. We need to do following to create a tag cloud:

1. On the **Select visualization type** page, click on the **Tag Cloud** option. This will open the index selection page.
2. Select the **metricbeat*** index pattern, as we want to create a tag cloud display using the Metricbeat Metricset data types. This will open the **New Visualization** screen.
3. Under **Metrics**, select the **Count** option in **Aggregation**.
4. Click on the **Tags** link under **Buckets**.

5. Choose **Terms** under **Aggregation**, and select **metricset.name** or any field you want to display.

6. Set the **Order By** and **Size** dropdowns as per your requirements. Add the **Custom Label** as `Name of metricset`.

7. Now click on the **Apply Changes** button to apply these changes, which will create the tag cloud type visualization, as shown in the following screenshot:

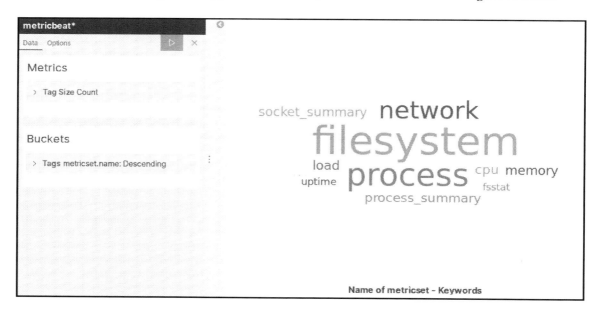

This way, using any field of the index, we can create the tag cloud, and then this visualization can be added to the dashboard.

Inspecting the visualization

We can inspect the visualization to see the actual data behind the graphical visualization. We can also see the statistics, such as the number of total hits, index pattern, query time, request time, and more, or the actual request JSON of Elasticsearch and the actual response JSON of Elasticsearch.

We can also download the formatted or raw CSV data from the inspect screen. We need to click on the **Inspect** link in the top-left to open the **Inspect** panel for the visualization. The following screenshot shows us the data view of **Inspect**:

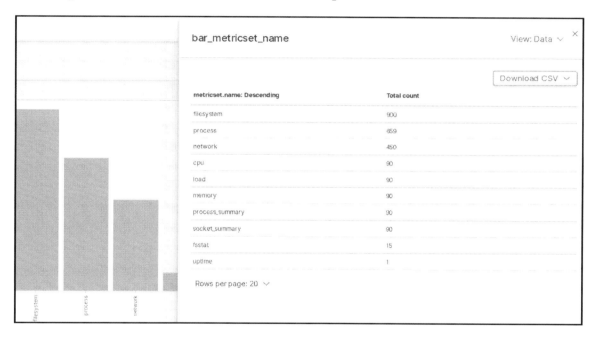

In the preceding screenshot, we can see the data behind the visualization using the **Inspect** panel. It is showing the actual data of the **metricset.name** field and its **Total count**. In the same way, we can inspect any graphical visualization in Kibana to know the data behind the visualization. We can also see the requests by selecting **View: Requests** from a dropdown in the top-right corner of the page. This opens a view, which is shown in the following screenshot:

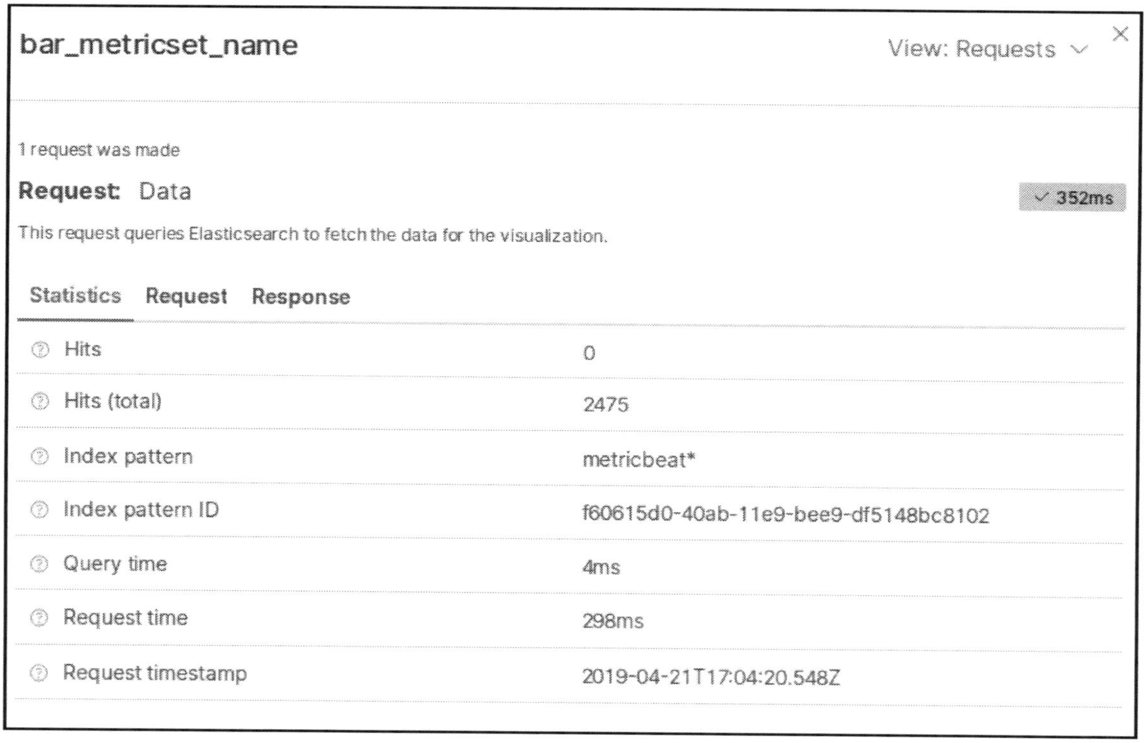

bar_metricset_name	View: Requests ∨ ✕

1 request was made

Request: Data

✓ 352ms

This request queries Elasticsearch to fetch the data for the visualization.

Statistics   **Request**   **Response**

⑦ Hits	0
⑦ Hits (total)	2475
⑦ Index pattern	metricbeat*
⑦ Index pattern ID	f60615d0-40ab-11e9-bee9-df5148bc8102
⑦ Query time	4ms
⑦ Request time	298ms
⑦ Request timestamp	2019-04-21T17:04:20.548Z

The preceding screenshot shows the **Statistics** of the request, where we can get to know the total hits, the index pattern used, the ID of the index pattern, the query time, the request time, the request timestamp, and more. We have the option to see the actual request made and the response received from Elasticsearch by clicking on the **Request** and the **Response** links. The following screenshot shows the request panel of the inspect screen, which shows the actual request query to Elasticsearch:

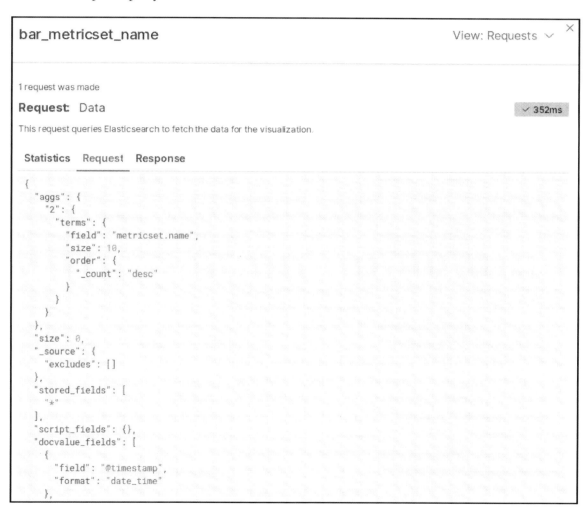

In the preceding screenshot, we can see the actual Elasticsearch query behind the visualization. This way, we can inspect any visualization in Kibana to know the data, request, response, and statistics behind it.

Sharing the visualization

Once the visualization is created, we can embed it on any web page using the **Share** option of the visualization. To share a visualization, we need to click on the **Share** button in the top-right corner of the page. This opens the **Share this visualization** popup with two options: **Embed code** and **Permalinks**. The **Embed code** option is there, using which we can copy the `iframe` code to integrate it on any web page.

There are two different options under **Embed code**; the first is **Snapshot**, using which we can save the current state of the visualization, and no change on current visualization after creating the snapshot will reflect this. Another option is **Saved Object**, which shows the most recently saved version of the visualization, as if we do an update in the visualization, it will be reflected in the shared version. We have the option of a short URL, using which we can create a short URL of the **Embed code**.

Let's say we want to embed the most recent link of the **bar_metricset_name** visualization, which shows the bar chart with different types of Metricsets on the **X-Axis** and **Total requests** on the **Y-Axis**. So, now, we need to click on the **Share** button and then click on the **Embed code** link, which opens the panel from where we can select the **Saved object** option, and then click on the **Copy IFrame code** button, which will copy the following `iframe` embed code for the visualization.

The following `iframe` code is the example code that is copied when we click on the **Copy IFrame code** button:

```
<iframe
src="http://localhost:5601/app/kibana#/visualize/edit/1cb98ab0-644a-11e9-9f
28-7f5f9c1f7a91?embed=true&_g=()" height="600" width="800"></iframe>
```

We can copy the preceding code and use it on any web page to display the visualization on the custom page. So, now, as we have the `iframe` code, let's create a web page called `kibana.html` by writing a very simple code:

```
<html>
<head>
<title>Kibana embedded visualization</title>
</head>
<body>
<h2>Kibana Visualization display</h2>
<h3>This is my custom web page</h3>
<iframe
src="http://localhost:5601/app/kibana#/visualize/edit/1cb98ab0-644a-11e9-9f
28-7f5f9c1f7a91?embed=true&_g=()" height="600" width="800"></iframe>
</body>
</html>
```

In the preceding code, we are creating a simple web page with `title` and `heading` with the `iframe` code to embed the Kibana visualization on this web page. After saving the HTML file, open it in a browser to display the web page, and it will show something like the following screenshot:

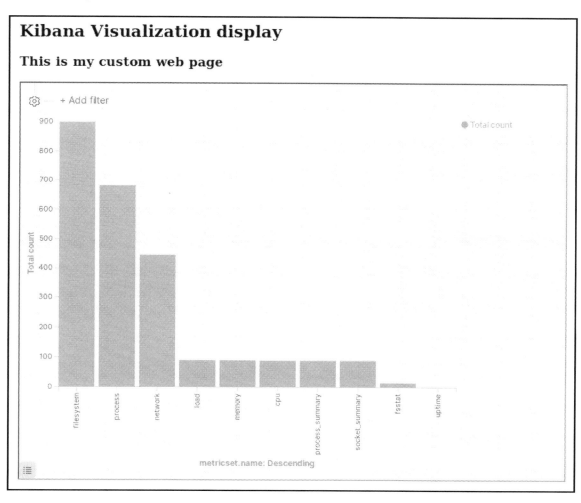

The preceding screenshot shows the HTML page with the embedded Kibana bar graph visualization. This way, we can embed any visualization in the HTML page, and we can show it inside the web page.

Creating dashboards in Kibana

So, we have covered how to create different types of visualizations in Kibana; now, let's see how we can integrate different types of visualizations to create the dashboard. Dashboards are quite useful, as they provide us with a single view to monitor the KPI. To create a dashboard in Kibana, we need to do the following:

1. Click on the **Dashboard** link from the left-hand menu, which will open the dashboards page with a list of the existing dashboards.
2. We can click on any existing dashboard to open the dashboard. But as we want to create a new one, click on the **Create new dashboard** button in the top-right corner of the page.
3. This will open a blank page with the message **This dashboard is empty. Let's fill it up!**.
4. Click on the **Add** button to add the visualizations; this will open **Add Panels** screen, as shown here:

In the preceding screenshot, we have the visualization and saved search options from where we can add already-saved visualizations or we can add new visualizations. We can search the visualization using the search box and can click on the name of the visualization to add that to the dashboard panel. In this way, we can add all those visualizations that we want to show on the dashboard panel.

Here is a link that has a screenshot of the dashboard view after adding some visualizations on the dashboard page: `https://github.com/PacktPublishing/Learning-Kibana-7-Second-Edition/tree/master/Images`

As visible in the screenshot, we have added a metric visualization, bar chart, pie chart, line chart, tag cloud, area chart, data table, and heatmap visualization to the dashboard. After creating the dashboard, we can do a lot of things, and the following are some options that we can perform with the dashboard:

1. We can save it by clicking on the **Save** link from the top-right links. After saving the dashboard, we can click on the **Edit** link to edit the dashboard. In edit mode, we can do the following things:
    1. Rearrange the visualization panels by dragging and dropping them into the desired location.
    2. Edit the visualization by clicking on the **Edit visualization** link under **Panel settings.**
    3. We can inspect individual visualization data by clicking on the **Inspect** link under the **Panel settings.**
    4. The visualization can be viewed in full screen by clicking on the **Full screen** link under **Panel settings.**
    5. We can change the label of the visualization by clicking on the **Customize panel** link under **Panel settings.**
    6. We can also delete any visualization from a dashboard by clicking on the **Delete from dashboard** link under **Panel settings.**
2. We can apply the dark theme, and we can hide/unhide panel titles or show/hide margins between panels by clicking on the **Options** link from the top-left links.

Sharing the dashboard

Once the dashboard is created, we can embed it on any web page by embedding the shared dashboard link. To share a dashboard, we need to click on the **Share** button in the top-right corner of the page. This opens the **Share this dashboard** popup with two options, **Embed code** and **Permalinks**. The **Embed code** option is there, using which we can copy the iframe code to integrate it into any web page.

There are two different options under **Embed code**; the first is **Snapshot**, using which we can save the current state of the dashboard, and no change on the current dashboard after creating the snapshot will be selected. Another option is **Saved Object**, which shows the most recently saved version of the dashboard, as if we do an update in the dashboard, it will be reflected in the shared version. We have an option of the short URL, using which we can create a short URL of the embedded code.

The following expression shows the embedded dashboard in HTML code:

```html
<html>
<head>
<title>Kibana embedded dashboard</title>
</head>
<body>
<h2>Kibana Dashboard Display</h2>
<h3>This is my custom web page</h3>
<iframe
src="http://localhost:5601/app/kibana#/dashboard/e0b13630-6467-11e9-9f28-7f
5f9c1f7a91?embed=true&_g=()" height="1000" width="1570"></iframe>
</body>
</html>
```

The preceding expression shows the HTML page where we have embedded the Kibana dashboard using the <iframe> tag. Here is a link that has a screenshot of the dashboard that displays the HTML page with the Kibana dashboard: https://github.com/PacktPublishing/Learning-Kibana-7-Second-Edition/tree/master/Images

The screenshot depicts a web page where we have embedded the Kibana dashboard. Using this embedded feature of Kibana, we can include the dashboard on any new or existing web page.

Generating reports

We can generate PDF or PNG reports from the dashboard in Kibana, as follows:

1. For that, we need to click on the **Share** link from the top-left menu and click on **PDF Reports** or **PNG Reports**, as shown in the following screenshot:

2. Once we have clicked on any of the report options, it will give us a message that the report is being generated and will be available in the **Management** option.
3. Now, to view or download the reports, we need to click on the **Management** link from the left menu and then click on the **Reporting** link under Kibana. This will open the following screen:

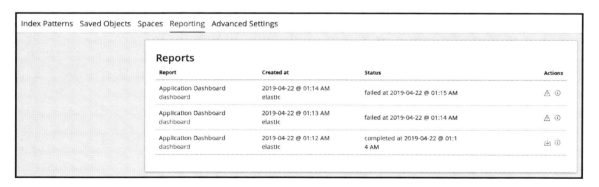

The preceding screenshot of **Reporting** will display all the reports that we have generated so far. We can download the reports from this listing by clicking on the download icon. This way, we can generate the reports from Kibana's dashboards or visualizations.

Summary

In this chapter, we covered the different types of visualizations and how to create them. We also covered data identification for visualizations and moved to a practical approach for creating some of them. We started by creating area charts, bar charts, and line charts, where we also covered how to convert one chart to another from the given options on the visualization page. Then, we covered pie chart creation and heat map creation, and then we created a data table and metric visualizations.

After these visualizations, we created a tag cloud to display a word cloud using an index field. After creating these visualizations, we inspected them using the inspect visualization option and shared them on a web page by embedding the `iframe` code of the visualization. We covered dashboard creation by adding each of the visualizations that we had seen so far. Then, we saw how to use the dashboard share option to embed the dashboard on a web page and to download the reports using the dashboard.

In the next chapter, we will cover **Dev Tools** and **Timelion**. These tools are very important in Kibana; using Dev Tools, we can execute Elasticsearch queries directly from Kibana, while using Timelion, we can play with time series data and create complex visualizations.

Section 3: Tools for Playing with Your Data

In this section, we will cover DevTools, under which we will discuss Console, Search Profiler, and Grok Debugger. Then, we will cover Timelion, using which we can play with time-series data. At the end of this section, we will discuss how we can create different Spaces in Kibana.

The following chapters will be covered in this section:

- Chapter 5, *Dev Tools and Timelion*
- Chapter 6, *Space and Graph Exploration in Kibana*

5
Dev Tools and Timelion

In this chapter, we will be discussing **Dev Tools** and **Timelion**, which are very important features of Kibana. Dev Tools has three main options that we can use for different operations: **Console**, **Search Profiler**, and **Grok Debugger**. Console helps us to interact directly with Elasticsearch, as we can run Elasticsearch queries on any index directly from the Kibana console.

It provides us the type hint, alignment, and option to copy the query as a cURL command, which we can directly paste to a Terminal to execute. Using Search Profiler under Dev Tools, we can profile the Elasticsearch query, and, using Grok Debugger, we can write the pattern to match the unstructured data, in order to convert it into structured data.

Timelion is a tool using which we can play around with time series data. We will cover how we can create different visualizations by chaining the Timelion functions over time-series data. Timelion also provides us with flexibility, where we can plot a graph using different Elasticsearch indices, which is not possible in Kibana Visualize.

Using Timelion, we can play around with the data and solve different queries; for example, if someone wants to see the difference between the current data and last week's data, we can plot them both on the same visualization. It makes it easy to figure out the differences, and we can easily know what the trend is. Timelion has many functions that provide us with the option to chain them together to create a complex visualization.

We are going to cover the following topics in this chapter:

- Introducing Dev Tools
- The Dev Tools Console
- Search Profiler
- Grok Debugger
- Introducing Timelion
- Building a metrics dashboard in Timelion based on time-series data
- A practical example of Timelion with some use cases

Introducing Dev Tools

Dev Tools is an important feature of Kibana where we have a console for running Elasticsearch queries, a search profiler to profile the Elasticsearch query, and Grok Debugger to create a grok pattern for extracting fields from unstructured data, such as log files. For accessing the Elasticsearch index in Kibana, we need to create the index pattern; however, using the Dev Tools console, we can directly run queries on any index of Elasticsearch.

The search profiler of Dev Tools provides details of each query with the query duration for each component of the query, along with the percentage of time consumed for each component. We can optimize the queries using this detail if any component is taking a long time.

Now we will cover these three features of Dev Tools in detail.

Console

Using the Dev Tools **Console**, we can execute all Elasticsearch queries and can see the results on the same screen. It provides us with suggestions, using which it is quite easy to construct a query. Apart from the type hint, we have the **Auto Indent** option, using which we can indent our queries. We can also copy the Elasticsearch query using the **Copy as cURL** option on the Dev Tools **Console**.

The following screenshot shows the **Console** view of Dev Tools. On the left-hand pane, we have the query, and on the right-hand pane, we have the result of the query:

In the preceding screenshot of the Dev Tools **Console**, we have two panes: one for constructing and executing the Elasticsearch query and one for viewing the result of the query. In the left-hand pane, we can type the Elasticsearch query, and, during this process, **Console** provides us with the type hint, using which we can easily construct the query. After creating the query, we can click on, Click to send request icon to execute the query, and once the query is executed, we can see the result in the right-hand pane.

After we click on the send request icon, we have the settings icon, which provide us three options, as shown in the following screenshot:

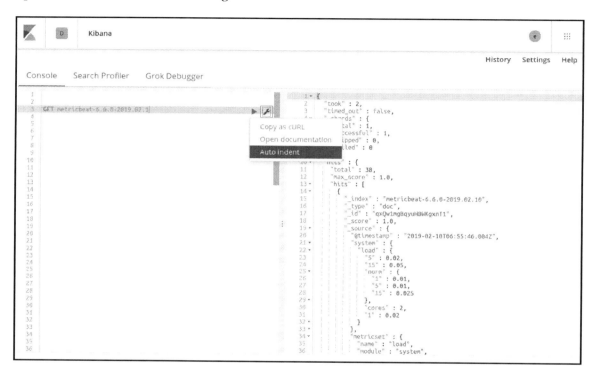

In the preceding screenshot, we can see the options under the settings for a query. So, there are three options under the settings, which are as follows:

- **Copy as cURL**: Using this option, we can copy the query as `curl`, as if we want to execute the query on a Terminal, then `curl` is the only option. So, we can construct the query on the Kibana **Console** and then can copy it as `curl` using the **Copy as cURL** option. The following expression shows a query where we are fetching the Metricbeat index data from the **Console** of Kibana Dev Tools:

  ```
  GET metricbeat-6.6.0-2019.02.1
  ```

  Now if we copy this query using the **Copy as cURL** option, then the same query from the Kibana **Console** can be converted into a `curl` query for fetching Metricbeat index data; see the following expression:

  ```
  curl -XGET "http://172.31.xx.xxx:9200/metricbeat-6.6.0-2019.02.1"
  ```

The preceding expression shows the `curl` query, which can directly be run on a Terminal to fetch the Elasticsearch data from the Metricbeat index.

- **Open documentation**: Using the **Open documentation** option, we can open the documentation page from the Elastic website. The documentation depends on the type of query we are trying to execute, so if we are running a `GET` query, then we can see the **Get Index** documentation of Elastic, and if we are opening the documentation from a `DELETE` query, then **Console** will open the **Delete Index** documentation page of Elastic. This way, we can directly open the documentation from the Kibana **Console** page in case of any doubt, just by clicking on the **Open documentation** link.
- **Auto indent**: The third option under settings is **Auto indent**, which is useful when we are constructing a complex query and the indentation of the query is not correct. By clicking on this option, we can easily indent the query.

Let's take the following example, where we have a query that is sorting the timestamp in descending order:

```
GET metricbeat-6.6.0-2019.02.10/_search
{
  "query":{"match_all":{}},
"sort":[{"@timestamp":
{
  "order":"desc"
}
}]}
```

In the preceding expression, the query is not indented properly, so if we try to indent it manually, then we need to check and fix everywhere. Now, using the **Auto indent** option, we can indent the query in a single click, which will transform the query, as shown in the following expression:

```
GET metricbeat-6.6.0-2019.02.10/_search
{
  "query": {
    "match_all": {}
  },
  "sort": [
    {
      "@timestamp": {
        "order": "desc"
      }
    }
  ]
}
```

The preceding expression is showing the auto indented query, which is easy to understand and debug. If we click on the **Auto indent** option again, it will indent the query in a compressed way, as shown in the following expression:

```
GET metricbeat-6.6.0-2019.02.10/_search
{"query":{"match_all":{}},"sort":[{"@timestamp":{"order":"desc"}}]}
```

The preceding expression shows the query in a compressed way. So, we have the option to expand the query or compress it using the **Auto indent** link under the settings.

Search profiler

The query profiler is a Kibana tool that comes under X-Pack, and using it, we can profile our queries and diagnose the queries that are performing poorly. It uses the Elasticsearch profiler API in the background, which returns a very large JSON blob that is not easy to analyze, but **Search Profiler** makes it easy for us by presenting this JSON data in the form of a visualization.

To profile a query in the Kibana **Search Profiler**, we need to click on the **Profiler** tab under Dev Tools, add the index name under the **Index** textbox, type the query into the left-hand pane, and then click on **Profile**, which will show the query profile result, as shown in the following screenshot:

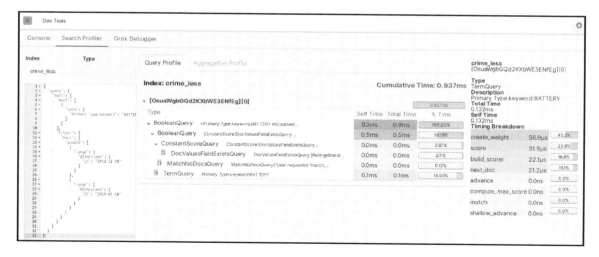

The preceding query shows the result of **Query Profile**, where we have added a query in the left-hand pane to the profile. This query is a Boolean query where we want to fetch all records where the primary type must be BATTERY and the timestamp should range from 2018-12-20 to 2019-01-10; see the following query:

```
{
  "query": {
    "bool": {
      "must": [
        {
          "term": {
            "Primary Type.keyword": "BATTERY"
          }
        }
      ],
      "filter": {
        "bool": {
          "should": [
            {
              "range": {
                "@timestamp": {
                  "gt": "2018-12-20"
                }
              }
            },
            {
              "range": {
                "@timestamp": {
                  "lt": "2019-01-10"
                }
              }
            }
          ]
        }
      }
    }
  }
}
```

In the preceding query, we are fetching data from the **crime_less** index of Elasticsearch using a term match and time range. We used to construct such queries for getting the results; however, using the query profiler, we can get an idea of how the query is performing and what the different areas where we can modify the query are. Now see the following screenshot with the query profiler result:

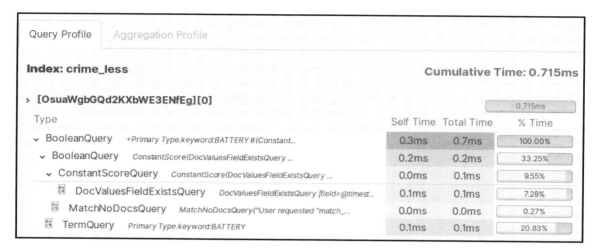

In the preceding query profiler result, we can see the different set of queries executed to perform the actual query. So, if we start looking at the screenshot, it first shows the name of the index and then the shard (with an ID of the node), under which we can see the type of queries being executed. We can click on the shard to expand the details, which show the **BooleanQuery** on the top hierarchy and then a **BooleanQuery**; after that, we have a **ConstantScoreQuery**, which shows **DocValuesFieldExistsQuery** in the hierarchy and **MatchNoDocsQuery** in parallel.

In parallel to the **BooleanQuery**, we have **TermQuery**. Now, if we elaborate on the outer **BooleanQuery**, which takes 100% of the time, it is now distributing its time in two main queries. First, **33.25%** with **BooleanQuery**, which checks the timestamp range and, second, **20.83%** with **TermQuery**, where we are matching the **Primary_type** term with the BATTERY value. Using these details, we can tweak the query to improve the performance after profiling through the **Search Profiler**.

We can use any complex query and then profile using the Kibana **Search Profiler** as it uses color to show the segments that are taking more time than the other segments of a query.

Aggregation profile

By default, we can see the **Query Profile** view if we try to profile any query using the Kibana query profiler, but we can also profile an aggregation query using the **Aggregation Profile** option of **Search Profile**, which is only enabled when we try to profile an aggregation query; see the following query expression:

```
GET metricbeat-6.2.2-2018.11.19/_search?size=0
{
  "aggs": {
    "rtt": {
      "stats": {
        "field": "metricset.rtt"
      }
    },
    "network_packet_in": {
      "stats": {
        "field": "system.network.in.packets"
      }
    },
    "network_cpu": {
      "stats": {
        "field": "system.cpu.cores"
      }
    }
  }
}
```

In the preceding expression, we are fetching the metrics aggregation for the rtt, network_packet_in, and network_cpu fields of the Metricbeat index, which represents the Metricbeat data. Now, if we type this query under **Search Profiler** and click on the **Profile** button, it will open a default **Query Profile** tab view; however, because we are profiling an aggregation query, we can get the **Aggregation Profile** option enabled.

If we click on the **Aggregation Profile** option, then it will open the following screen:

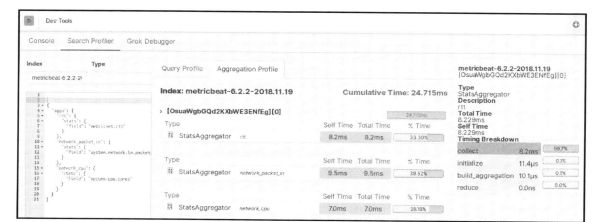

In the preceding screenshot, we can see the index name as **metricbeat-6.2.2-2018.11.19**, and then the shard with the node ID, under which we can see all three aggregations. Here, the first is `rtt`, the second is `network_packet_in`, and the third is `network_cpu`. To know the profile details of any aggregation, we need to click on the link, and we can see the details on the right-side of the page. This way, we can profile any aggregation query as well, using the **Aggregation Profile** option of Kibana Dev Tools.

Grok Debugger

Kibana grok pattern is a tool that helps us to construct grok patterns. We can use grok patterns to parse unstructured data such as different logs, which can be any web server log, such as Apache or nginx, any database log, such as MySQL, or syslog logs. These logs are written for us to see whether there is an issue in the system or whether we want to know what is causing the problem.

 Grok expressions are basically a pattern-matching syntax, which can be used to parse arbitrary text and convert that into a structured format.

But the unstructured format of logs makes it difficult to fetch any details in an easy way. By creating a grok and applying it in Logstash, we can easily convert the unstructured data into structured data, which can easily be searched and analyzed. But it is never easy to write a **Grok Pattern** and test it every time by executing the Logstash configuration to check whether we are getting the intended results.

Kibana grok patterns makes this process quite easy as we can simulate the **Grok Pattern** execution and see the result on the same page. To create a **Grok Pattern** in Kibana, we need to click on the **Grok Pattern** tab on the Dev Tools page, which will open the following screen:

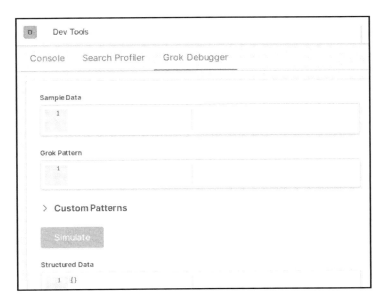

The preceding screenshot shows the **Grok Pattern** page, where we have three segments, **Sample Data**, **Grok Pattern**, and **Structured Data**, which are described as follows:

- **Sample Data**: Here, we use to type the unstructured **Sample Data** from any log such as Apache, MySQL, syslog, or any other arbitrary data. We can write the **Grok Pattern** to create **Structured Data** using this data.
- **Grok Pattern**: Here, we write our actual **Grok Pattern**, and it matches the sample data value. Once we write our **Grok Pattern**, we can click on the **Simulate** button to see the result.
- **Structured Data**: Once the **Grok Pattern** is written and we click on the **Simulate** button, the **Structured Data** can be seen under the **Structured Data** text area. In case of any issue, an error message can be displayed, and we won't be able to see anything under the **Structured Data** text area.

Now, look at this example where we have a log with the following structure, and we have an IP address, request method, URL, total bytes, and duration to serve the page:

```
127.0.0.1 GET /mytestpage.php 11314 0.011
```

In the log file, we have the line-wise entry of these logs, which is quite difficult to search and find in case of any anomaly; however, if we can push this log into Elasticsearch, then we can leverage the full text search benefit of it and drill down to get any minute detail from the log file. But, again, because it is unstructured data, how can we search if the method is GET or POST or the URL is abc.html? For that, we need to extract this unstructured data through the mapping to convert it into **Structured Data**.

For this conversion, we use grok patterns, and by applying the grok plugin into Logstash, we can push the **Structured Data** into Elasticsearch or any other output source. Now, let's take the example of a **Grok Pattern**, using which we can extract the preceding log:

```
%{IP:client} %{WORD:method} %{URIPATHPARAM:request} %{NUMBER:bytes}
%{NUMBER:duration}
```

In the preceding expression, we are matching the log entry to the **Grok Pattern**. So, when we try to simulate this pattern against the sample data, it gives us the following result:

```
{
        "duration": "0.011",
        "request": "/mytestpage.php",
        "method": "GET",
        "bytes": "11314",
        "client": "127.0.0.1"
}
```

In the preceding result, we can see that the unstructured log entry has been changed in structured key-value pared JSON. In this way, we can simulate the grok pattern against sample data in the Kibana **Grok Debugger**, and, once it is working, we can use the pattern in our Logstash configuration to process the actual data against the pattern.

Now, let's take a little more complex data such as Catalina logs from a Java application:

```
2019-02-19 13:53:53.080 WARN 27408 --- [Executor-870113]
o.s.web.client.AsyncRestTemplate : Async POST request for
"https://ohionewstore.com" resulted in 401
```

The preceding sample data has been taken from the catalina.out log file, which captures the Java application logs. This is a little complex from the previous example, as there are different segments that we need to extract and match with the field names. See the following pattern, which we have written to match the preceding sample Catalina log entry:

```
%{TIMESTAMP_ISO8601:timestamp}%{SPACE} %{LOGLEVEL:level}
%{NOTSPACE:sessionid} --- %{NOTSPACE:thread} %{NOTSPACE:source} %{SPACE}:
%{GREEDYDATA:message}
```

In the preceding pattern expression, we are handling the field mapping along with spacing and dashes (---) to extract the unstructured data into structured data. After simulating the pattern against a sample Catalina log entry, we can get the following result:

```
{
    "level": "WARN",
    "sessionid": "27408",
    "thread": "[Executor-870113]",
    "source": "o.s.web.client.AsyncRestTemplate",
    "message": "Async POST request for \"https://ohionewstore.com\" resulted
in 401",
    "timestamp": "2019-02-19 13:53:53.080"
}
```

This way, we can create our own grok pattern here, and once it runs successfully, we can apply it for a complete set of data to convert it into a structured form. The following screenshot shows an example of Catalina log extraction using **Grok Pattern**:

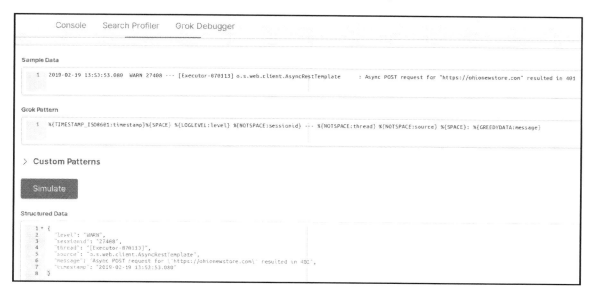

In the preceding screenshot, we can see the Catalina log sample data under the **Sample Data** textbox, and then we have the pattern under the **Grok Pattern** textbox. In the **Structured Data** text area, we can see the structured data, which is generated after clicking on the **Simulate** button. This way, using Dev Tools, we can do some of the very important stuff in an easy way.

Next, we are going to cover Timelion.

Timelion

As per Elastic, Timelion is the clawing, gnashing, zebra-killing, pluggable time series interface for everything. So, Timelion is basically a visualization tool, which works on time series-based data, and we can plot data from different sources against the time in a single visual representation.

If we talk about Kibana Visualize, then we can use only one index for creating a single visualization; however, using Timelion, we can plot using multiple Elasticsearch indices. Hence, it makes it easy to view data from a different tangent on a single time frame to understand the similarity between them and to know how they are dependent on each other.

In Elastic Stack Version 7.x, the **Timelion** link is not available by default, but we can enable it by setting the `timelion.ui.enabled` option under the `kibana.yml` file. We can open the **Timelion** link by clicking on the **Timelion** link from the left-hand menu; the following screenshot shows the default **Timelion** view:

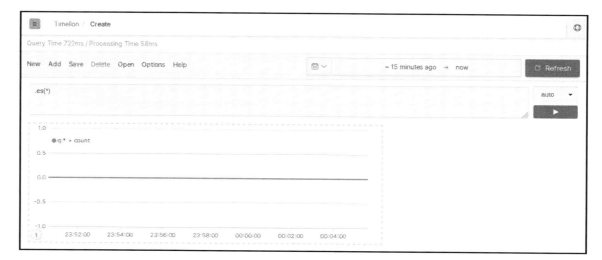

The preceding screenshot shows the default **Timelion** view, where we have the **Timelion** query bar where we can write different expressions; by default, it shows `.es(*)`, which refers to Elasticsearch. Under the query bar, we have the visualization, which represents the expression in visual form. We have an apply button, using which we can execute the expression.

Timelion provides us a way, where, using simple expression language, we can retrieve time-series data, perform mathematical calculations, and change the label or color of the visualization. Timelion also provides us the help link in the top-left corner, using which we can open the reference document where we can see the list of available functions and what exactly they do.

The following screenshot shows the help page of **Timelion**:

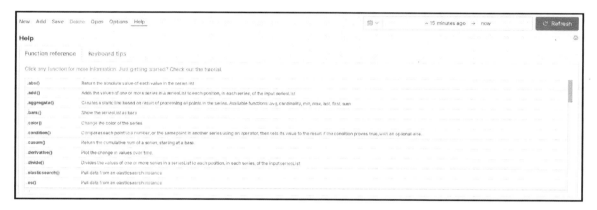

The preceding screenshot shows the default **Function reference** tab of Timelion's **Help** view. Here, we can see a list of the available functions, which we can use for the Timelion expression. We can chain these functions to write a complex expression, which can generate a complex visualization. Also, we can write different expressions on the same plot by separating them with a comma (,). In this way, we can generate a visualization using multiple plots, which all represent a different set of data against the time series.

We also have keyboard shortcuts for Timelion, which we can open by clicking on **Keyboard tips** under the **Help** page of Timelion, which opens the following page:

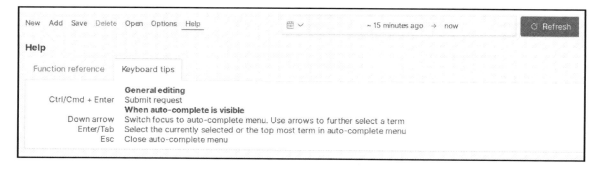

The preceding screenshot shows the keyboard shortcut options available in Timelion. So, now, we will cover the different functions of Timelion, and we will see some practical examples by using Metricbeat data, as all beats generate time-series data, which can easily be worked on the Timelion. Metricbeat provides us with details of system metrics, such as memory usage, CPU usage, and more. So, let's start generating some visualizations though Timelion functions using Metricbeat data.

.es()

The `.es()` function is the shortcut of the `.elasticsearch()` function, which is used to fetch data from Elasticsearch and plot it against time on the x axis. It fetches the time series-based data from Elasticsearch indices and draws it against the time on the x axis. By default, it queries all the indices of Elasticsearch if we do not provide any specific index name explicitly.

The .es() function shows the plot on the basis of the document count in the index. The .es() function supports different parameters that we can pass to the function as required. Each parameter has a predefined format that we need to follow if we are not providing the name of the parameter; otherwise, the .es() function won't be able to recognize the parameter. For the .es() function, we have the following parameters:

- q: By providing the q parameter, we can add a query string to filter the data.
- index: By providing the index parameter, we can specify the name of the index pattern to be used for the data plot. If we miss this parameter, Elasticsearch will pull data for all index patterns.
- metric: By providing the metric parameter, we can apply different metrics such as sum, min, max, percentile, and more, on any field. We need to provide the metric name followed by the field name, for example, sum:system.memory.used.bytes.
- split: Using the split parameter, we can split a field with a limit. For example, if we want to show the top five hostnames, then we can pass hostname:5.
- offset: By providing the offset parameter, we can retrieve the data based on the offset expression, for example, if we want to show the data of the last five days on the chart, which would appear as it is happening now. To show the data of the last five days, we need to provide the -5d value for the offset.
- fit: The fit parameter provides us the algorithm, using which we can fit the empty values using different options such as average, nearest, none or scale, and more.
- timefield: The .es() function picks the default time field for the index, which we can change by providing the time field parameter to use for the x axis.

Now, if we want to plot the metricbeat index data and we want to plot 35 minutes old data, then we can do so in the following way:

```
.es(q=*, index=metricbeat*, timefield=@timestamp, offset=-35m)
```

In the preceding expression, we are using four parameters of the .es() function:

- q to match everything
- index to pull metricbeat index only
- timefield to select @timestamp as the time field
- offset to show the data for the past 35 minutes

The following screenshot shows the result of the preceding expression:

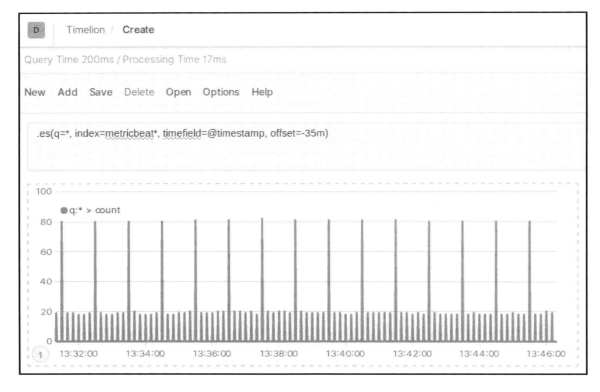

The preceding screenshot shows the visualization that we have created using the .es() function. Once the visualization is created, we can save it by clicking on the **Save** link in the top-left section of the page, in the same way we can save any Timelion visualization.

Using the **Options** link, we can set the number of rows and columns on the page. Using the **Add** link, we can add one more Timelion query textbox with a visualization. Using the **Open** link, we can open any already saved Timelion visualization.

.label()

By chaining the `.label()` function, we can add or change the label of a series. By using percentages, we can get the reference of the existing label. By default, Timelion shows the label on the visualization by picking the given expression, which is sometimes quite difficult to understand on a graph. To solve such situations, we can use the `.label()` function, as it is important to add a meaningful label to the series. Using the following expression, we can add the label to any series:

```
.es(q=*, index=metricbeat*, timefield=@timestamp,
offset=-35m).label('metricbeat 35 minutes old data')
```

In the preceding expression, we are adding the `label` to the previous `.es()` expression.

.color()

By applying the `.color()` function, we can change the color of any series. In the preceding `.es()` expression, we can apply the `.color()` function to change the Metricbeat series color to green. Timelion applies different colors for different expressions automatically, and we can change that color using the `.color()` function as per our requirement. See the following screenshot, where we have changed the color of the previous Timelion visualization:

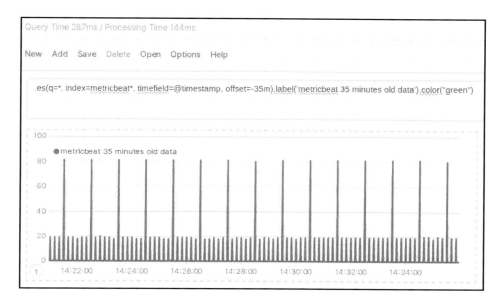

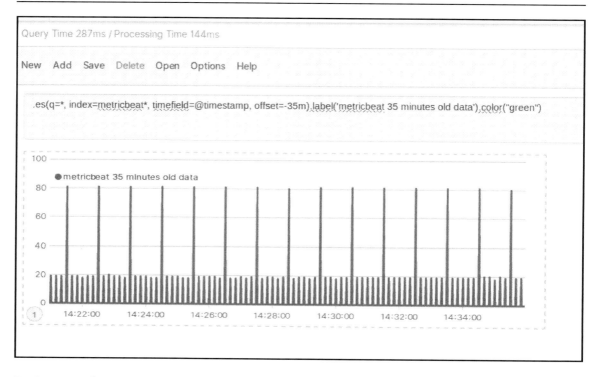

In the preceding screenshot, we can see that the series color has changed to green after applying the .color() function of Timelion with the parameter as green.

.static()

Using the .static() function, we can draw a static horizontal line on the chart with a given value. We can use this static line to show a threshold on the graph. We can use the label method to add the label to the added plot on the graph. In the following expression, we are adding the .static() function to show the threshold value:

```
.es(index=metricbeat*, metric=count:event.duration), .static(50, "Threshold
Value").color('red')
```

In the preceding expression, we are adding the static line to display the threshold in red, which is set to 50. This way, we can validate the event.duration count value against this threshold value. The following diagram shows the static line in red:

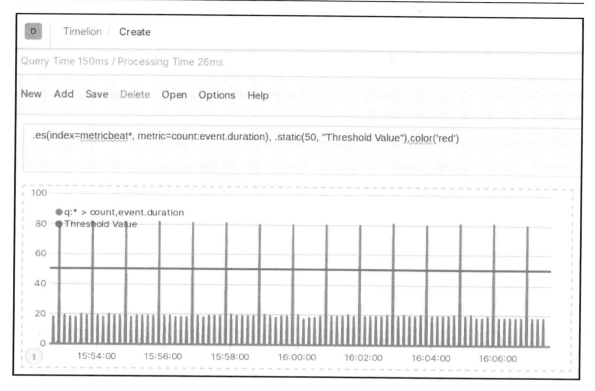

In the preceding screenshot, we can easily validate our graph against the threshold value, which is shown in red. It is quite handy, and we can easily add them to any chart.

.bars()

Using the `.bars()` function, we can convert the chart from a line type to a bar type representation using the same time-series data. See the following expression:

```
.es(index=metricbeat*, metric=count:event.duration).bars().label('event
duration'), .static(50, "Threshold Value").color('red')
```

In the preceding expression, we are chaining the `.bars()` function after the `.es()` function to convert it into a bar chart. In the following screenshot, we have changed the view of the Metricbeat data line to a bar by chaining the `.bar()` function at the end of the first expression:

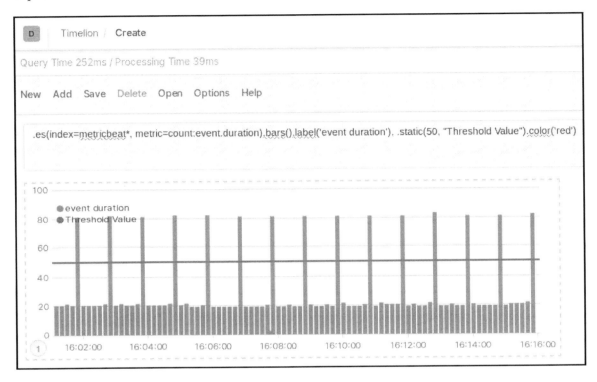

In the preceding screenshot, we can see that the same Metricbeat data has been converted from a line chart to a bar chart. By chaining the `.bars()` function to any Timelion expression, we can convert that into a bar chart.

.points()

As with the `.bars()` function, we have a `.points()` function, using which we can change the chart series display as points instead of the line type. These functions are very handy, as they are easy to use, and we can replace or remove them at any time to revert the chart display. See the following expression:

```
.es(index=metricbeat*, metric=count:event.duration).points().label('event
duration'), .static(50, "Threshold Value").color('red')
```

In the preceding expression, we have added the `.points()` function after the `.es()` function. After executing the preceding expression, we can see the following screen:

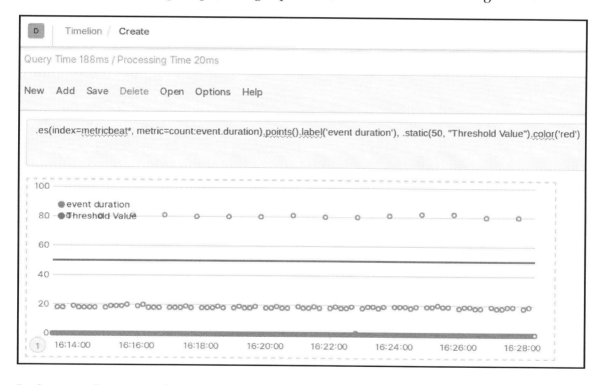

In the preceding screenshot, we can see the same chart as a point type display. We can use the point type chart if the chart looks condensed and it is difficult to understand anything, as it only shows the start and end points, which makes the chart display more clear.

.derivative()

The .derivative() function is used to plot the difference in value over time. It shows the derivative of a time series, which is the slope of the curve. As we have seen in other functions, we also need to chain the .derivative() function with the existing function.

The following screenshot shows the derivative of the time series for Metricbeat data for the count of the event.duration field:

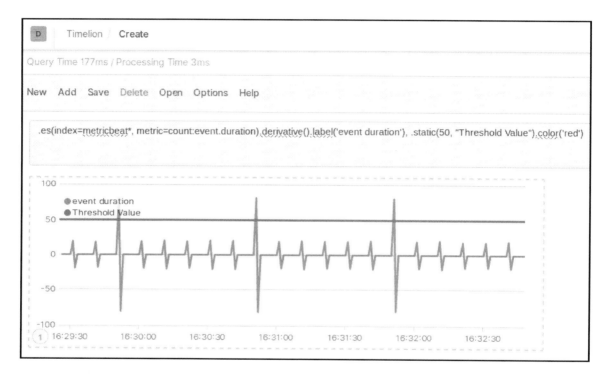

In the preceding screenshot, we can see the derivative for the `.es()` expression value. This way, we can apply the `.derivative()` function to any function for showing the derivative of that particular expression.

.holt()

The `.holt()` function basically samples the series data from the beginning and then forecasts the future trend of series data using different optional parameters. We can also use it for anomaly detection. It has different parameters such as `alpha`, which ranges from 0 to 1; if we increase the `alpha` value, the new series will closely follow the original series, and if we lower the alpha value, it will make the series smoother.

Then comes the `beta` value, which also ranges from 0 to 1, and increasing it will make the rising/falling line longer, while decreasing the `beta` value will make this quickly learn the new trends. After `beta`, we have `gamma`, which also ranges from 0 to 1, and if we increase it, it will give more importance to the recent reasons; if we lower it, then it will give less importance to the recent series data that is similar to giving more importance to the historical data.

Then, we can provide the season such as the `duration` to pick for repeating, such as `1w` for one week. If we provide the season, then we can also set the last parameter, which is a sample to set the number of seasons to pick for data sampling. The following expression shows a simple `.holt()` function implementation:

```
.es(index=metricbeat*, metric=count:event.duration).label('event
duration').holt(0.1,1), .static(50, "Threshold Value").color('red')
```

In the preceding expression, we have added the `.holt()` function after the `.es()` function to see the trend; the following screenshot shows the actual chart created using the preceding expression:

In the preceding screenshot, we can see the current trend in the form of a smooth representation of the chart.

.trend()

If we want to see what the trend of the data is, then we can apply the `.trend()` function, which creates a plot for the trend using the regression algorithm. To explain the data trend, I am going to use the sum metric of the `system.process.memory.size` field of Metricbeat. So, for applying the trend to the preceding series, we need to apply the `.trend()` function in the expression, as follows:

```
.es(index=metricbeat*, metric=sum:system.process.memory.size
).label('system process memory size').trend()
```

After executing the preceding expression, we can get a trend plot showing the data trend based on the history. The following screenshot shows a plot that is showing the current trend for the series:

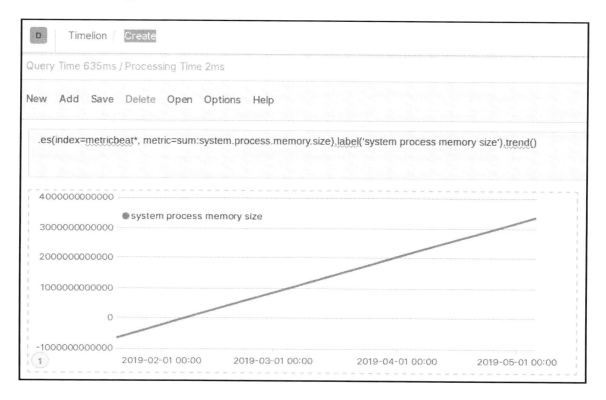

The preceding graph shows the trend of the data going up in the last 15 weeks. This trend can be created for any data series just by chaining the expression with the .trend() function.

.mvavg()

If we are getting lots of spikes in a graph, then it is quite difficult to get the idea about how the data series is plotted. To solve these kind of issues, we can use the moving average function, which calculates the average of a series in a regular time interval and then plots the chart on the basis of the calculated value. Now look at the following example:

```
.es(index=metricbeat*, metric=sum:system.process.memory.size).label('system
process memory size')
```

Using the preceding expression, we are trying to plot the metric for the sum of the `system.process.memory.size` field, which creates the following chart:

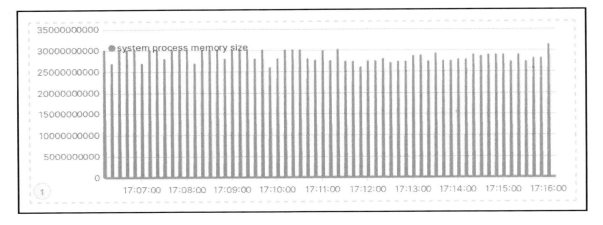

The preceding screenshot shows the graph for the sum of the `system.process.memory.size` field, but this graph has a lot of spikes, which are very difficult to understand. To solve this issue, we can apply the moving average to the expression to smooth the graph. Refer to the following expression:

```
.es(index=metricbeat*, metric=sum:system.process.memory.size).label('system
process memory size').mvavg(30s)
```

In the preceding expression, we are chaining the `.mvavg()` function with 30 seconds as a parameter, which we generate by moving the average every 30 seconds. After executing the preceding expression, we will get the following chart:

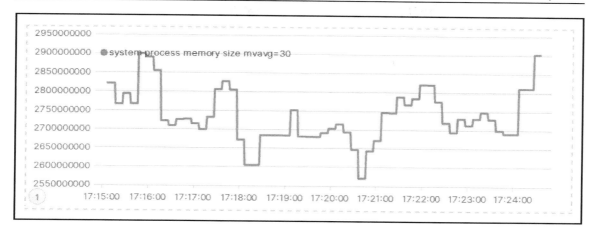

The preceding screenshot shows the chart after applying the moving average of 30 seconds. Now this chart is quite easy to understand, and, in the same way, we can apply the moving average to any of the existing expressions.

This way, we can use the Timelion functions and can chain them together to get the desired results. These were some of the important functions that I have covered here; apart from them, there are many other functions that you can refer to from the **Help** option of the Timelion page. There is one more important aspect of Timelion, and that is comparing the current data to older data in the same data visualization graph.

A use case of Timelion

There can be different use cases of Kibana Timelion, but here I am going to explain a case where you will want to check the variations in a data series. If you want to know what is happening, then put the current and two-minute-old data on the same frame and check the deviation. It provides a very easy way to identify the variations. See the following expression:

```
.es(index=metricbeat*, metric=sum:system.process.memory.size).label('system
process memory size').color(green).mvavg(10s).label('current data') ,
.es(index=metricbeat*, metric=sum:system.process.memory.size,
offset=-2m).label('system process memory
size').color(blue).mvavg(10s).label('2 min old data')
```

In the preceding expression, we are using two sets of the `.es()` function representing the same field: `system.process.memory.size`. The first one shows the current data, while the second one shows the two-minutes-old data, as we have passed the `offset` parameter with a value of `-2m`, which is fetching the two-minute-old data. We are also differentiating them from each other by using different colors; for the first set of data, we are using green, while for the second, we are using blue.

Refer to the following screenshot, which shows the output of the preceding expression:

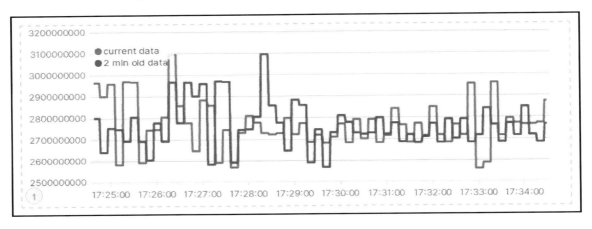

In the preceding screenshot, the green shows the current data, while blue shows two-minute-old data. Using this chart, we can easily get the difference at any point of time. This is quite helpful, as not only a single type of data but also different types of data can be plotted against the same time frame.

Summary

In this chapter, we have covered Dev Tools and Timelion, which are quite useful tools in Kibana. We started with Dev Tools, using which we can do multiple things. After this, we covered the different options of Dev Tools, such as Console, using which we can execute Elasticsearch queries and can get the response on the same page. Then, we covered the search profiler, using which we can profile any Elasticsearch query by getting the details of the query components.

Then, we covered Grok Debugger, where we created the Grok pattern to parse sample data through which the unstructured sample data was converted into structured data. This structured data was then used for data analysis or visualization.

After Dev Tools, we covered Timelion and the different functions that are available in Timelion. Like the `.es()` function to set the Elasticsearch data source, it has different parameters, such as index, metric, split, offset, fit, time field, and more.

After that, we learned about other functions such as `.label()` to set the label for a data series, `.color()` to change the color of the plot, `.static()` to create a static line on the *x* axis, and `.points()` to convert the graph into a point display. Then, we discussed the `.derivetive()` function, which plots the differences in value over time and the `.holt()` function, which forecasts future trends or gets anomalies in the data. We also covered the `.trends()` function to get the data trends, and the `.mvavg()` function to apply a moving average on the expression. Finally, we created the chart to compare the current series with the two-minute-old series at the same time frame on the *x* axis.

In the next chapter, we will cover the graphs and space in Kibana. Using Graph, we will find the similarities in the dataset, and while using Space, we will create separate space for different users.

Space and Graph Exploration in Kibana

In this chapter, we will learn about using Kibana spaces, which can be used to organize saved objects, dashboards, and visualizations through role-based access control. Spaces help us to arrange secure and well-managed dashboards, visualizations, and saved objects for end users. By default, Kibana provides a space that is known as the default space. We can create, edit, delete, or customize these spaces and, once a space is created, we can provide user access to it so that users can see their own spaces and access things within that particular space.

Following spaces, we will learn about Kibana graphs and explore how Elasticsearch index items are related to each other. In particular, we will learn how indexed terms are connected and which connections are more meaningful. We will use Kibana graphs for different use cases, such as for recommendation engines and fraud detection. Here, a graph is essentially a form of network in which we can explore related terms in an index.

In this chapter, we will cover the following topics:

- Kibana spaces
- Creating a space
- Editing a space
- Deleting a space
- Switching between spaces
- Creating a Kibana graph
- Analyzing relationships using saved objects between spaces
- Restricting space access
- Kibana graphs
- Differences with industry graph databases
- Advanced graph exploration

Kibana spaces

With Kibana spaces, we can organize saved objects and dashboards by categorizing them in the form of separate spaces. These spaces provide the option to separate things for different users. Once we create a space, Kibana asks us to choose the space we want to use when we are logged in. After navigating inside the space, we can see the saved objects, dashboards, and more. Under X-Pack, we can provide specific access to spaces for different user roles using the security feature. Spaces are enabled by default in Kibana, and we can disable them using the **xpack.spaces.enabled** option in Kibana settings by changing it to **false**. Kibana creates a default space that we cannot delete, but we can customize it as per our requirements.

We can manage the Kibana space from the **Management** page. To do so, we need to click on the **Spaces** tab on the **Management** page, which will open the following page:

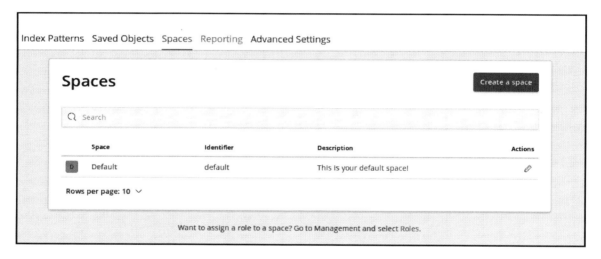

The preceding screenshot shows the default Kibana **Spaces** page that lists the available spaces, an edit option, and a button to create a new space.

Creating a space

Now, let's take a look at how we can create a new space in which we can restrict the things a user can view or access:

1. We can create a space by clicking on the **Create a space** button on the **Spaces** page in **Management**. This will open the following page:

The preceding screenshot displays the **Create a space** page that we can use to create a new space. Here, we need to fill in the **Name**, **URL Identifier**, and **Description** details.

2. Once these details are filled in, we can click on the **Create space** button to create the space. The following screenshot shows the form to **Create a space**:

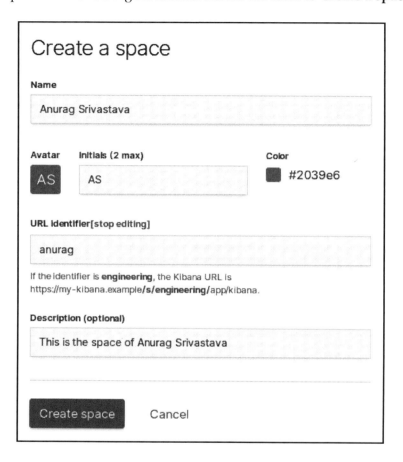

In the preceding screenshot, I have added the **Name** and, following this, we have the option to edit the **Avatar**, where we can pick the two characters that we want to be displayed plus the background color.

3. Then, we have the **URL Identifier** that we can modify as per our requirements. Finally, at the bottom of the page, we have a **Description** in which we can add the space description.
4. After clicking on the **Create space** button, we can save this space and see it listed on the **Spaces** page, as shown in the following screenshot:

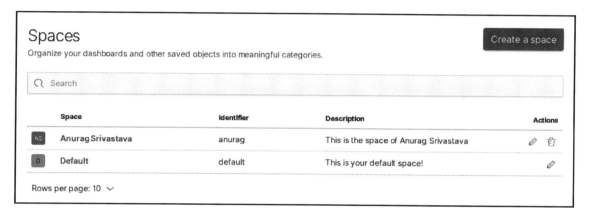

The preceding screenshot shows the listing of the spaces; here, we can see the **Space** name, **Identifier**, **Description**, and **Actions**. Under **Actions**, we also have options to edit and delete the space. Note that the delete option is only for those spaces that we have created, as we cannot delete the default space of Kibana.

Editing a space

Once a space is created, we can edit it to modify the **Name**, **Avatar**, and **Description** details. However, note that the **URL Identifier** is non-editable. After changing these details, we can click on the **Update space** button to update the details. The following screenshot shows the **Edit space** page where we can update the details:

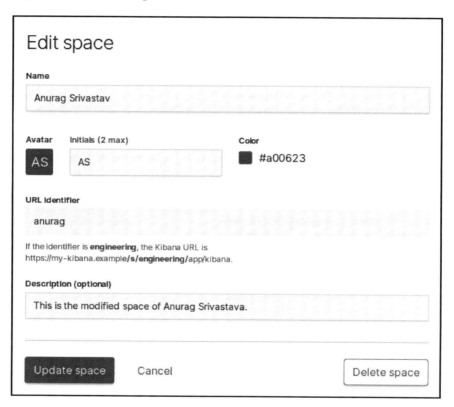

In the **Edit spaces** page, you can see that we have edited **Name**, **Avatar**, and **Description**. In this way, we can modify any space after creating it.

Deleting a space

We have covered how to create a space and how to modify it, so let's now learn how to delete a space in Kibana. We can delete the space from two places. First, we can navigate to the **Spaces** listing page and then click on the delete icon next to the space row; second, we can go to the **Edit spaces** page and click on the **Delete space** button. After clicking on the delete button from either of these pages, we will get the following pop-up message. To confirm that you want to delete the space, you will need to type in the space name again:

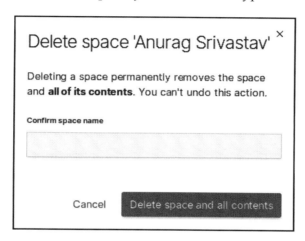

The preceding screenshot shows the delete space confirmation page with the message: **Deleting a space permanently removes the space and all of its contents. You can't undo this action.** Underneath this message, we are asked to confirm the space name by typing it into the textbox. After typing in the space name, we can click on the **Delete space and all contents** button to finally delete the space.

Switching between spaces

We can switch between our created spaces by clicking on the current space icon in the top-left corner of the page. This opens the **CHANGE CURRENT SPACE** pop-up box. From here, we can click on any space that we want to switch to; take a look at the following screenshot:

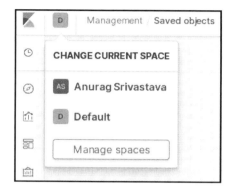

In the preceding screenshot, we can see two different spaces, From here, we can click on any of the spaces in order to load it. It changes the Kibana URL by appending the space name, for example, `hostname/s/SPACE-NAME/app/`.

Moving saved objects between spaces

So far, we have learned how to create the space, modify it, delete it, and switch it in Kibana. Now, let's take a look at how we can move a saved object from one space to another. For this, we need to use the **Import/Export** UI in Kibana to first export the saved object from one space and then import it to another space.

To export the saved object from a space, we need to perform the following steps:

1. Click on the **Management** link in the left-hand menu and click on the **Saved Objects** option under Kibana. This will open the list of saved objects.
2. Select the saved object that you want to export and then click on the **Export** button. This will save the exported JSON file.

3. Now, switch to the space that you want to import the exported saved object to and then navigate to the same **Saved Objects** page.

4. Click on the **Import** link in the top-right corner of the page. This will open the **Import saved objects** popup.

5. Click on the **Import** link and select the exported JSON file. Then, enable or disable the **Automatically overwrite all saved objects?** option.

6. Now, click on the **Import** button to import the saved object.

7. This will import the saved object and will show a success message with the total number of imported objects.

8. Click on the **Done** button to see all of the imported saved objects.

In this way, we can move saved objects from one space to another.

Restricting space access

So, we have created a space and learned how to move the saved object from one space to another. However, the main feature of a space is to restrict users to their own spaces. Now we are going to take a look at how you can restrict users to work in their own space under Kibana, so that we can configure the things a user can see. This requires multiple steps; for example, first, you need to create a role that provides the desired access rights for that space. Then, that role has to be assigned to a user. I have created and called the space **anurag srivastava**, so let's create a role and user and then demonstrate how to restrict that user.

Creating a role to provide access to a space

So far, we have learned how to create a space, modify it, and delete it. But these things are irrelevant unless we provide role-based access on spaces. Using role-based access, we can restrict access for different users through different roles. The security feature is freely available from Elastic 7.1 onward; however, for older versions, we will need to enable X-Pack. To create a role to restrict access to a single space, we need to perform the following steps:

1. Click on the **Management** link from the left-hand menu. Then, on the **Management** page, click on the **Roles** link in **Security**. This will open the **Create role** page. Here is a link that has a screenshot you can refer to: `https://github.com/PacktPublishing/Learning-Kibana-7-Second-Edition/tree/master/Images`

In the image provided in the link, we can see that the page is mainly grouped under three sections: the first contains the **Role name**, the second is used to set the **Elasticsearch** options, and the third is to set the **Kibana** option for different access.

2. Provide the role name, for example, **anurag_space**, and leave the **Elasticsearch** section as it is.
3. In the **Kibana** section, set **Minimum privileges for all spaces** to **none**.
4. Under **Higher privileges for individual spaces**, select the space name from the spaces drop-down menu, for example, **Anurag Srivastava**. In the **Privilege** drop-down menu, select **all**. We can choose the **all**, **none**, or **read** options there.
5. Now, we can click on the **View summary of spaces privileges** link to see the current access settings for the space; take a look at the following screenshot:

In the preceding screenshot, we can see that, for the **Anurag Srivastava** space, we have all of the privileges. Whereas, for the **Default** space, the privilege setting is set to **none**. After the confirmation, we can click on the **Create role** button to save the role. In this way, we can create any role by providing different access settings for different spaces.

Creating a user and assigning the space access role

We have created the role with space access, so let's now create a user and assign the role so that we can restrict the user to access a single space only. To create the user, we need to perform the following steps:

1. On the **Management** page, click on the **Users** option under the **Security** options. This will open the **Users** page.
2. Click on the **Create new user** button; this will open the **New user** form.
3. Fill in the **Username, Password, Confirm password, Full name**, and **Email address** details.
4. In the **Roles** drop-down menu, select the created role, that is, **anurag_space**:

In the preceding screenshot, we can see the **Create user** form. Here, we can provide the basic user details along with the assigned roles. We are creating a user with a single role, **anurag_space**, so that the user can only access a single space in Kibana:

5. Click on the **Create user** button to create the user.
6. After clicking on the button, the user can be created. We will then be redirected to the users listing page, where we can see the newly created user.
7. The user has been created; to verify this, we can log in using this new user.

Checking the user space access

Kibana spaces are configured in such a way that we can separate saved objects or indices in a different space for users. In the case of a normal or default user login, Kibana asks us to select the space we want to access, as follows:

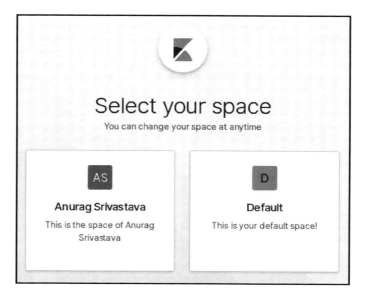

The preceding screenshot shows the default Elastic user after logging in. Here, we need to select any space in order to proceed further. However, as we have assigned the **anurag_space** role to the newly created user, this role has full access to only a single space, which is **anurag srivastava**. So, let's try to log in through this new user; after logging in, we see the main page of Kibana instead of an option to pick the space. Even if we click on the default space icon in the top-left corner, it does not show the option to switch to the other available spaces:

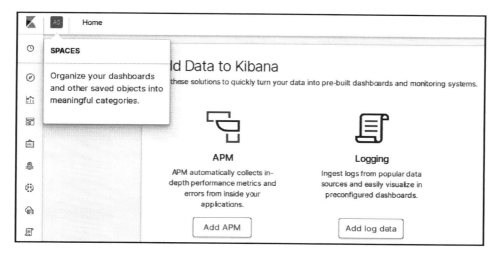

The preceding screenshot shows the default view of the user with access to only a single space through the Kibana role. In this way, we can customize access to different spaces through a role and then assign that role to either existing or new users. Let's take an example where you have different saved objects but different users need different saved objects that you cannot share with other users. Using spaces and role-based access, we can easily configure this. We can create dashboards inside the spaces to secure them from outside the space access.

Kibana graphs

Elastic graph comes with a new API in Elasticsearch and a new UI in Kibana that offers a totally different approach to exploring data: rather than addressing data through the angle of value aggregation and narrowing them down by filtering to discover patterns, the graph allows you to play with vertices (that is, the terms indexed in Elasticsearch) and connections (that is, how many documents share the terms in the index) and map out significant relations.

Differences with industry graph databases

In some graph technologies, search results are based on the popularity of records. This means that, if we take music data that describes people and what they listen to and then try to search for **Mozart** to get related artists, we will get the following results. For the sake of simplicity, I have represented the result rows in the form of green boxes, with the related artist on top of it. The bigger the green box, the more popular the artist. In our search example, the first row will naturally be **Mozart**, but then we'll find **Coldplay**, **The Beatles**, and, somewhere at the end, we should find **Bach**.

Coldplay and **The Beatles** are pretty popular across the dataset, and they will most likely be present in every single graph exploration. However, their popularity is diluting the signal we are looking for, that is, classical music artists related to **Mozart**; they are creating noise. They are called **super-connected entities** because data points are never more than a couple of hops away from them; they will always end up touching a super-connected entity, as shown in the following diagram:

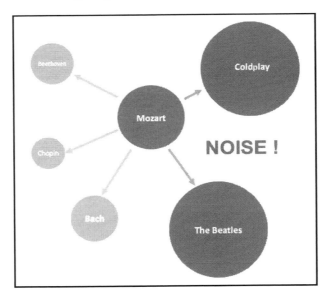

Their inclusion is usually what happens in mainstream graphing technology; this is because it's not their job to calculate the relevancy and the significance of the results. The good news is that it's exactly what Elastic graph is good at.

When we throw terms in the Elasticsearch indices, it naturally knows which data is the most interesting and leverages that to build the graph.

Elasticsearch looks for the reinforcement of many documents to show the strength/relevancy of the connection.

Creating a Kibana graph

Using a Kibana graph, we can find how different Elasticsearch index items are associated with each other. We can check and see how indexed terms are connected and which connections are stronger. Through Kibana graphs, we can solve different problems such as recommending things or detecting fraud.

A graph is essentially a form of network that we can use to find related terms in an index. Each term that we add to the graph is known as **vertices** and the association between the two vertices is known as the **connection**. We can add different fields as vertices and can customize them with different colors and icons to make the graph more readable. Additionally, we have a search box where we can put in any search criteria after adding all of the vertices, to generate the connection between the vertices in the form of a graph view. Now, we are going to explore how to do graph analytics in the Elasticsearch index. Using this, we can explore the connections between different terms of the Elasticsearch index. Here, we will take the example of popular baby names data, which has been taken from the Data.gov website (`https://catalog.data.gov/dataset/most-popular-baby-names-by-sex-and-mothers-ethnic-group-new-york-city-8c742`). This is open data so we can freely download the data and use it.

The format of the data contains `Year of Birth`, `Gender`, `Ethnicity`, `Child's First Name`, `Count`, and `Rank`. The following example shows a snippet of the actual CSV data:

Year of Birth Count	Rank	Gender	Ethnicity	Child's First Name
2016 172	1	FEMALE	ASIAN AND PACIFIC ISLANDER	Olivia
2016 112	2	FEMALE	ASIAN AND PACIFIC ISLANDER	Chloe
2016 104	3	FEMALE	ASIAN AND PACIFIC ISLANDER	Sophia
2016 99	4	FEMALE	ASIAN AND PACIFIC ISLANDER	Emily
2016 99	4	FEMALE	ASIAN AND PACIFIC ISLANDER	Emma

The preceding dataset only displays the initial five lines of the actual CSV data that I have downloaded from the Data.gov website for popular baby names, but the actual file (`Popular_Baby_Names.csv`) contains 11,345 records.

We have covered index creation using `Popular_Baby_Names.csv` in `Chapter 3`, *Business Analytics with Kibana*, using Logstash.

So, here, we are going to use the same Elasticsearch index: **popular-baby-names**. In this index, we have popular baby names from different ethnicities; so, using this data, we will create a graph to understand the relation between the `Child's First Name` field and `Ethnicity`.

To perform the graph analytics on the popular baby names index, we need to perform the following steps:

1. We need to click on the **Graph** link in the left-hand menu link of **Kibana**.
2. In the **Select index pattern** drop-down menu, select the **popular-baby-names** index pattern.
3. Now, click on the plus icon to add a field source for the vertices and filter it using `Child's First Name`. Then, click on the **Add** button to add it, as follows:

The preceding screenshot shows the screen to add the vertices for graph analytics. Here, we are adding the `Child's First Name` field of the **popular-baby-names** index.

After clicking on the **Add** button, it opens the field customization screen from where we can change the **Color** for vertices representation on the graph, change the **Icon** for the vertices, and change the **Max terms per hop** value. Additionally, there is a **Remove** button that we can use to remove the vertices from the graph display; take a look at the following screenshot:

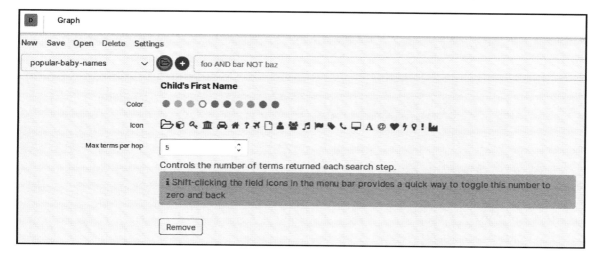

In the preceding screenshot, we can see the customization option for the `Child's First Name` field. We can customize it if we want to do so:

4. Again, click on the plus icon to add `Ethnicity` as another graph vertices, in the same way that we did for `Child's First Name`.

5. In the search box, type in any value such as the name of a child, that is, **tenzin**, and then click on the **Search** button; this will open the following view:

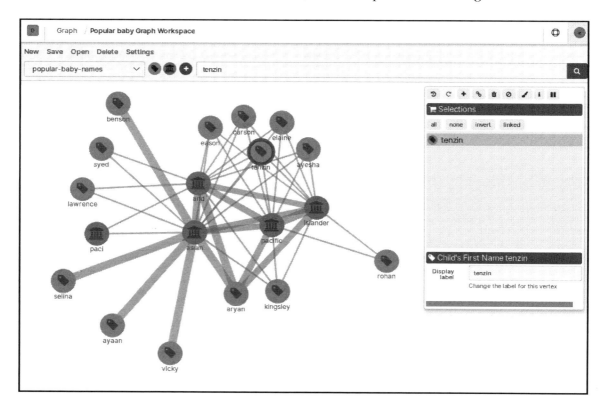

In the preceding screenshot, we can see the graph view of the **popular-baby-names** index where we are trying to explore the relationship between names and ethnicity.

The right-hand side box provides us with a different option to play with the graph view. Take a look at the top icons in the box; the first option is to undo, the second option is to redo, and the third option is a plus icon. This is used to expand the selection; we can select any vertices and click on the plus icon to expand it further.

Next to this is the link icon that is used to add links between existing terms; then, there is a delete icon to remove the vertices from the workspace.

The sixth link is there to blacklist the selection from returning to the workspace, and the seventh is to apply custom styles on the selected vertices. The eight option is to drill down further, while the last (ninth) option allows you to play or pause the layout:

The preceding screenshot shows the top icons in the right-hand side box on the graph page. In this way, we can create the graph view using the index pattern.

Advanced graph exploration

We have created the graph view using the **popular-baby-names** index. Now we can analyze the relationship between `Child First Name` and `Ethnicity`. What we are trying to find out is how child names are related to different ethnicities as, in this graph, we can see some names that are connected to many ethnicities, such as **tenzin**.

If we want to know how the name **tenzin** is connected to a different ethnicity, then we need to click on the icon of the name **tenzin**, and then click on the **linked** button under the **Selections** heading in the right-hand options box, which lists all of the linked ethnicities, including **islander**, **and**, **asian**, and **pacific**:

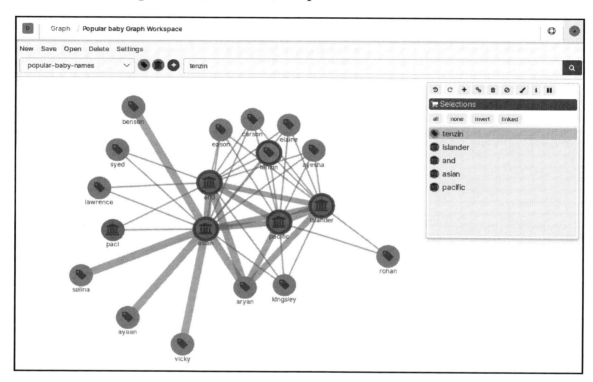

The preceding screenshot shows the relationship between the name **tenzin** and the different ethnicities where this name is found. In this way, we can identify the relationship between different vertices; you can see the highlighted icons on the graph view along with the listing on the right-hand options box. Using the **invert** button, we can invert the selection at any time. We can also see how vertices are connected with each other by clicking on the connecting lines.

Let's assume that we want to know how the name **aryan** is associated with the **asian** ethnicity. To find out, we can click on the line connecting the name **aryan** to the **asian** ethnicity and view the connection in the right-hand side options box under **Link summary**:

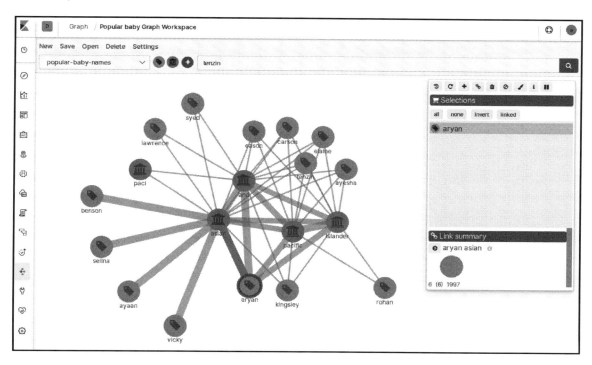

In the preceding screenshot, we can see how the name **aryan** is associated with the **asian** ethnicity. The **Link summary** box shows that there are **6** documents where the term **aryan** is available, while **1997** documents have the term **asian**. Additionally, if we talk about the similarity between them, then there are **6** documents where we have both terms.

So, we can get the exact analytics about the connection of two vertices using Kibana graph analytics. In this way, we can create a graph view for any index and then analyze the relationship between different vertices to find out more about their relationship and how they are associated with other vertices.

Summary

In this chapter, we learned about Kibana spaces and graphs; these are two very important features in Kibana. We started with Kibana spaces and learned how they can be used to separate saved objects and dashboards from different users. Then, we discovered how to create a space, edit it, and then delete it. Following this, we looked at how to switch between different spaces.

After that, we explored how to move saved objects between spaces and how to restrict space access by creating roles. Then, we looked at graphs; we were introduced to Kibana graphs and learned how to create a graph. After graph creation, we used the example of the **popular-baby-names** index and explained how to analyze relationships using a Kibana graph.

In the next chapter, we will cover Elastic features in more detail. We will cover security, monitoring, reporting, alerting, and other features that provide us with various benefits.

Section 4: Advanced Kibana Options

In this section, we will introduce the Elastic Stack, and cover its features, including security, reporting, monitoring, alerting, and machine learning. Then, we will cover machine learning, APM, and Canvas in detail.

The following chapters will be covered in this section:

- Chapter 7, *Elastic Stack Features*
- Chapter 8, *Kibana Canvas and Plugins*
- Chapter 9, *Application Performance Monitoring*
- Chapter 10, *Machine Learning with Kibana*

7
Elastic Stack Features

In this chapter, we are going to cover Elastic Stack features (formerly packaged as X-Pack) and how they impact the default setup of Elastic Stack. When we install Elastic Stack, it comes with all the basic features that we can extend by extending the basic license. It provides multiple features that are quite important, such as security, monitoring, alerting, reporting, machine learning, and many more.

For using the Elastic Stack features, we need to purchase the license; however, we can start a 30-day free trial to check all its features. So, if we talk about them in a little detail, then security is very much a necessary feature as we want to protect our Elastic Stack setup. By creating roles and users, we can differentiate our spaces, dashboards, saved objects, and so on with different roles that can be assigned to different users as per requirements.

Then, we have monitoring, using which we can monitor our Elastic Stack from a central place inside Kibana. It displays the cluster health and details such as rate of indexing, rate of search, and so on. We can check the details of Elasticsearch indices, nodes, and overview, and so on. Also, using monitoring, we can check the Kibana overview with details of instances. Using reporting, we can generate PDF or image-based reports from dashboards or visualization. Using alerting, we can configure the alert on a certain threshold, and can route emails or Slack messages whenever the values cross the threshold. Then, we have machine learning, using which we can check anomalies in the data and predict future trends.

Here, we will be discussing the following features of Elastic Stack:

- Security
- Monitoring
- Alerting
- Reporting

Security

Using Elastic Stack security, we can secure the stack with controlled access to the users. We can secure the access of dashboards, visualizations, and saved objects through spaces and Elastic Stack security. Using the Elastic Stack security feature of X-Pack, we can secure our cluster by password-protecting the data. We can easily apply the role-based access control on our Elastic Stack setup. There are basically two things that come under Elastic Stack security users and roles.

Using roles, we can control Elasticsearch and Kibana access by customizing the index access, space access, and so on. Under users, we can create and modify the users and can assign them the created roles to restrict their access. We are going to cover the roles and users in detail here, although they were covered in the last chapter, but that was restricted to Kibana spaces only. So here, we are going to cover the details of users and roles under the security feature of X-Pack.

 From Elastic Stack version 7.1, the security feature is freely available and we don't need to purchase the license for it.

Roles

Using roles, we can control the access of Elasticsearch and Kibana components that a role can or cannot access. For example, in Elasticsearch, we can control different cluster privileges such as **monitor, manage, manage_security**, and so on, and we can also control the **Run as privileges** and can provide it to any role.

Then, we have index privileges to restrict the role for certain indices only, and we can also grant read access to specific documents. For Kibana, we can set minimum privileges for all spaces and higher privileges for individual spaces for a role. This way, we can restrict to a role on the Elasticsearch and Kibana level. To create a role, we need to do the following:

1. Click on the **Management** link from the left menu of Kibana, which will open the **Management** page.
2. Now, click on the **Roles** link under the **Security** option, which will open the **Roles** page with a listing of existing roles; please refer to the following screenshot:

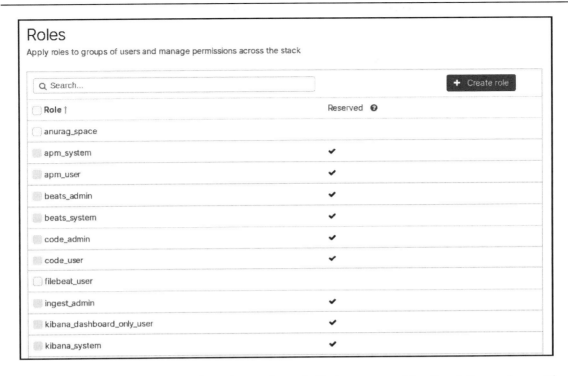

The preceding screenshot shows the role listing page with all existing roles, with a search option to search any specific role.

3. We need to click on the **Create role** button to create a new role, this will open a new page with three sections, the **Role name** section, the **Elasticsearch** section and the **Kibana** section.

4. In the **Role name** text box, we need to write the name of the role. Here, we should provide a name that is meaningful and using which we can easily see know what this role is doing. So here, I want to create a role for the Metricbeat index, hence the name `metricbeat_access`.

5. In the Elasticsearch section, we have options such as **Cluster privileges**, **Run As privileges**, and **Index privileges**.

6. For **Cluster privileges**, I am going to provide the **monitor** option as I only want the role to monitor clusters without any edit privileges.

7. For **Run As privileges**, we can pick any existing user, so here we can select any existing user or it can be left blank.

8. Under **Index privileges**, we can select any index, so here we can pick the **metricbeat*** index pattern with **all** privileges.

9. Under **Granted fields** we can add * for all. If we want to add more index for privileges, then we can click on the **Add index privilege** button; see the following screenshot:

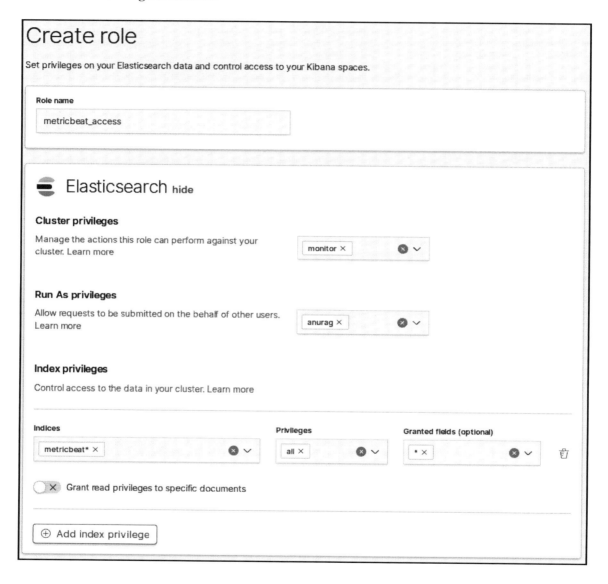

The preceding screenshot shows the **Create role** screen where we can add the **Role name** and can set the access for **Elasticsearch**. After the **Elasticsearch** section, we have the **Kibana** section using which we can set access for Kibana spaces. Now, let's cover the role setting for Kibana:

1. Under the **Kibana** section, we can set the **Minimum privileges for all spaces** as **read** so that the user with this role can read any space data on Kibana.
2. For the **Higher privileges for individual spaces**, we can set the space name, such as **Anurag Srivastava**, and privileges to **all** so that user with this role can access everything for the selected space.
3. We can click on **Add space privilege** in case we want to add more space privileges for the role; refer to the following screenshot:

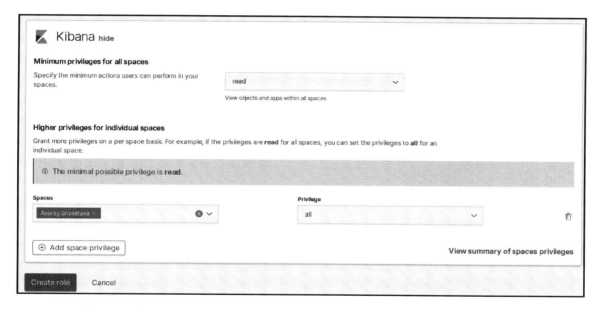

The preceding screenshot shows the **Kibana** section of role creation in Kibana. Here, we can control how different spaces can be accessed. We can control how a user will access all spaces in Kibana and how he/she will access the specific space in Kibana so we can restrict the user to **none**, **some**, or **all** spaces in Kibana.

4. Now, click on the **Create role** button to save the role. This will open the role list page with the newly create role. So this way, we can create any role to restrict the access for the Elasticsearch cluster, index, and so on and for Kibana spaces. After creating the required roles, we can create the users and can assign them the roles so that role-based access can be provided to different users.

5. We can click on the **Role name** on the list page to open the role in edit mode, where we can modify the role. We can also delete any role by selecting it and then by clicking on the **Delete** button. This was the role management of Kibana; now, let's cover user management.

Users

Through the **Users** option, we can handle the user management for Elastic Stack. We can create users, edit users, and delete users, and can assign the roles to the users. So for securing the stack, we need to create the role as well as the users so that as per the requirement we can create different users with different sets of roles. To create the users, we need to do the following:

1. We need to click on the **Management** link from the left menu of **Kibana**, which will open the **Management** page.
2. Now, click on the **Users** link under **Security** to open the users listing page; see the following screenshot:

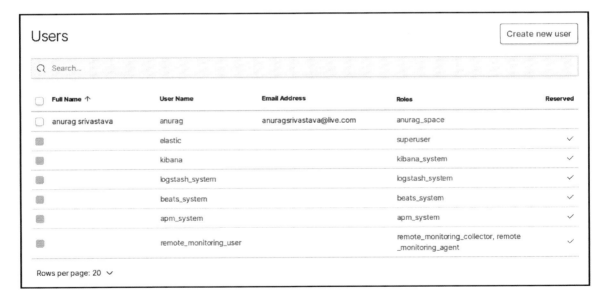

The preceding screenshot shows the default page of **Users** with a listing of existing users.

Now, click on the **Create new user** button on the user listing page. This will open the **New user** page:

1. Fill **Username**, **Password**, **Confirm password**, **Full name**, **Email address**, and select the **Roles.**
2. After filling all those details, click on the **Create user** button; see the following screenshot:

The preceding screenshot shows the **New user** form, where we can add user details, assign **Roles**, and click on the **Create user** button to save the user. This will add the user, and we can see the newly created user on the user listing page.

This way, we can create a new user in Kibana and can assign any available role. From the user listing page, we can click on the assigned **Role name**, which will open the role edit page, where by clicking on the username link we can open the user edit page. From the user edit page, we can modify the **Full name**, **Email address**, **Roles**, and **Password**. We can also delete the user from this user edit page by clicking on the **Delete user** link; see the following screenshot:

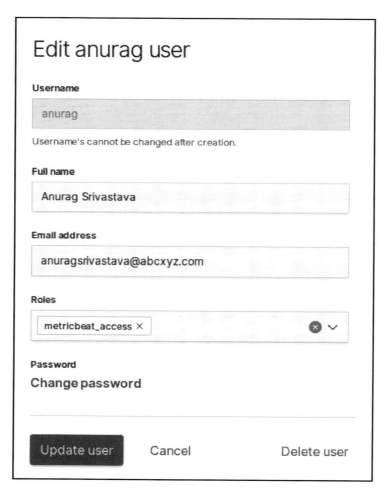

The preceding screenshot shows **Edit anurag user**, where we can edit the user details, change the role, or delete the user. We can delete the user by clicking on the **Delete user** link on the user edit screen or by clicking on the **Delete user** button on the user listing page after selecting the user. After clicking on the delete link, it shows a confirmation popup showing a message that **This operation cannot be undone.**

We need to click on the **Delete** button on this confirmation popup to delete the user; see the screenshot:

The preceding screenshot shows the confirmation popup, which comes after clicking on the user **Delete** button. This way, we can create roles and users to enable the security for your Elastic Stack.

Monitoring

Elastic Stack monitoring provides a feature with which we can get the insight of Elasticsearch, Logstash, and Kibana operations. All of the monitoring metrics are saved in Elasticsearch, which are displayed on Kibana UI under **Stack Monitoring**.

Under **Monitoring**, we can see the Elasticsearch cluster **Overview** with **Version**, **Uptime**, and **Jobs** details; here, we can get the details about the search rate, indexing rate, search latency, and so on. We also get node details such as disk availability, JVM heap size, its status with CPU usage, load average, JVM memory, total shards, and so on.

Under **Indices**, we can see the documents count, disk usage, primary shard count, and replica shard count, and so on. The following screenshot shows the **Monitoring** page, which can be opened by clicking on the **Stack Monitoring** link from the left menu of **Kibana**:

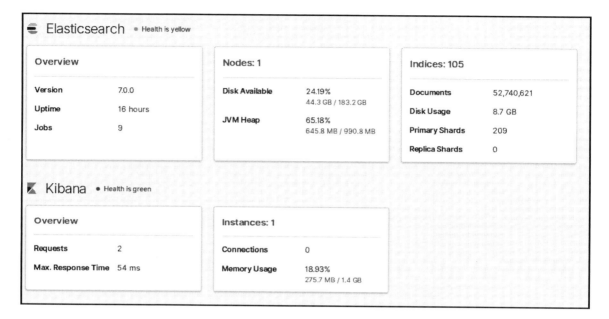

The preceding screenshot shows the Elastic Stack **Monitoring** page, where we can see the **Elasticsearch** and **Kibana** monitoring details. Now, let's see what we can monitor under **Elasticsearch**, and what is in **Kibana**.

Elasticsearch Monitoring

Under Elasticsearch **Monitoring**, we have three sections: **Overview**, **Nodes**, and **Indices**. The **Overview** is there to tell us the monitoring overview for Elasticsearch, such as the version of Elasticsearch, uptime, and total running jobs. If we click on the **Overview** link, it opens the detail page where we can see the summary with status, number of nodes, indices, memory consumption, total shards, unassigned shards, number of documents, and data size.

We can see the graphs of **Search Rate**, **Indexing Rate**, **Search Latency**, and **Indexing Latency**. It also shows the shard activity; please refer to the following screenshot:

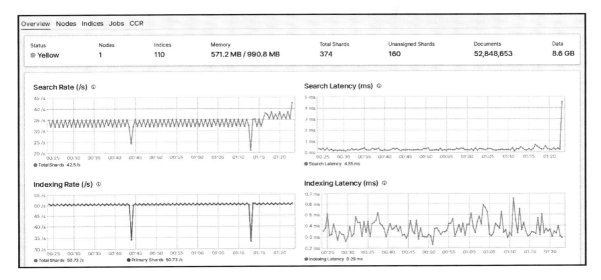

The preceding screenshot shows the Elasticsearch **Overview** detail view. The **Nodes** block shows us the count of nodes, available disk percentage with an actual utilization count, and JVM heap percentage with actual utilization.

We can click on the **Nodes** link to open the detailed view, where we can again see the summary and then a listing with node **Name**, **Status**, **CPU Usage**, **Load Average**, **JVM Memory**, **Disk Free Space**, and the total number of **Shards** in the node; please refer to the following screenshot:

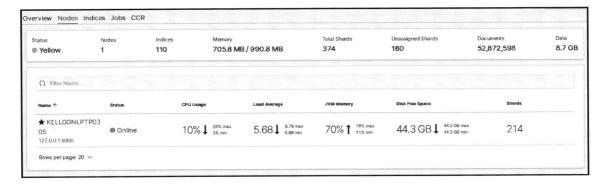

The preceding screenshot shows the detail view of **Nodes** link under Elasticsearch **Monitoring**. We can click on the node name link to see a further details page, where we can see two tabs with **Overview** and **Advanced** options; in both tabs we can see the summary with **Status**, **Transport Address**, **JVM Heap**, **Free Disk Space**, **Documents** count, **Data** size, number of **Indices**, number of **Shards**, and **Type** of node (master, data, and so on).

On the **Overview** tab, we can see the graphs with **JVM Heap (MB)**, **Index Memory (MB)**, **CPU Utilization (%)**, **System Load**, **Latency (ms)**, **Segment Count**, and **Shard Legend**; see the following screenshot:

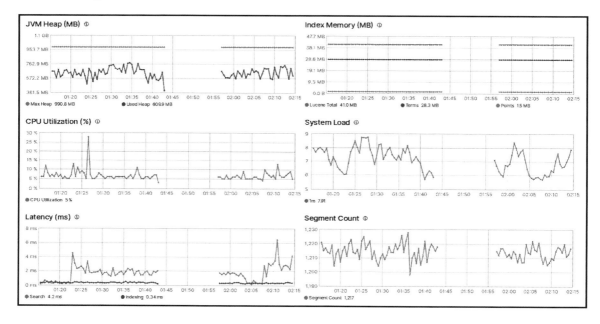

The preceding screenshot shows the **Overview** tab view of the **Elasticsearch** node. We can click on the **Advanced** tab to see a detailed view of the node. It shows graphs with **GC Count**, **GC Duration**, **JVM Heap**, **CPU Utilization**, **Index Memory**, **Indexing Time**, **Request Rate**, **Indexing Threads**, **Read Threads**, **C Group CPU Performance**, **C Group CFS Stats**, and **Latency**. Then, we have the **Indices** block, which shows the count of indices, documents, disk usage, primary shard count, and replica shard count as well.

We can click in the **Indices** link to open the detailed view, which shows the summary and a list of all Elasticsearch indices. The index list shows **Name**, **Status**, **Document Count**, **Data Size**, **Index Rate**, **Search Rate**, and **Unassigned Shards** count for all indices; please refer to the following screenshot:

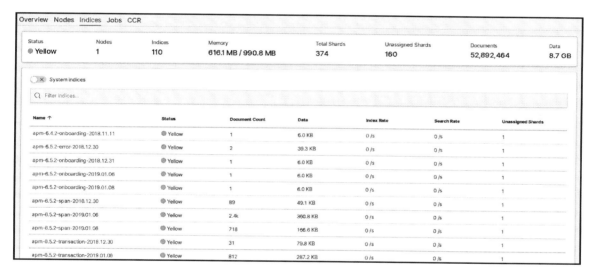

The preceding screenshot shows the list of indices along with their status and other metrics. Now, let's see what we can monitor in Kibana.

Kibana Monitoring

If we talk about stack monitoring for Kibana, then it basically shows the Kibana health with two blocks to show **Overview** and **Instances**. The **Overview** shows the number of requests and the max response time. We can click on the **Overview** link to open the detail view, where it shows a summary with **Status**, number of **Instances**, **Memory** utilization, the total number of **Requests**, **Connections**, and **Max. Response Time**, and graphs for **Client Requests** and **Client Response Time** in **ms**; refer to the following screenshot:

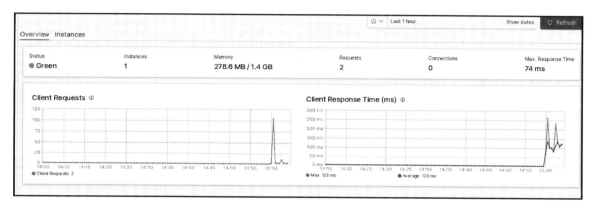

The preceding screenshot shows the **Overview** detail page of Kibana **Monitoring**; here, we can see the summary with two graphs that show the **Client Requests** and **Client Response Time**. Apart from the **Overview**, we have the **Instances** block, which shows the total number of Kibana **Instances**, **Connections**, and **Memory** usage.

We can click on the **Instances** link to see the detailed view, where we can see the instance **Name**, **Status**, **Load Average**, **Memory Size**, **Requests**, and **Response Times**; see the following screenshot:

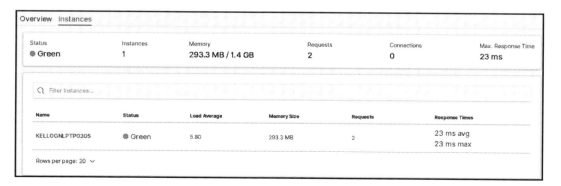

The preceding screenshot shows the instance detail of Kibana with status, name, and other metrics. We can click on the instance name to open the detailed view of the Kibana instance. Here, we can see the summary with **Status**, **Transport Address**, **OS Free Memory**, **Version**, and **Uptime**. Following the summary, we can see the graphs for **Client Requests**, **Client Response Time** in **ms**, **Memory Size** in **GB**, **HTTP Connections**, **System Load**, and **Event Loop Delay** in **ms**. Please refer to the following screenshot, which shows the graphs for **Client Requests**, **Client Response Time**, **Memory Size**, **HTTP Connections**, and so on:

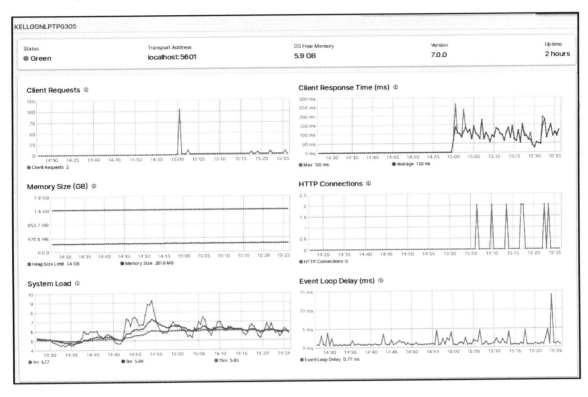

The preceding screenshot shows the Kibana **Instance** detail with summary and graphs. This way, we can monitor the Elastic Stack and its details, using which we can tweak it to take the full potential of the stack. Using these graphs, we can get an idea of how the system is performing and can identify the peaks and reasons behind those peaks.

Alerting

Alerting is a way to get notified for any event that is important to us. We can configure the alert if any field value crosses the threshold value, which we can set as per the requirements. In Kibana, we can notify using **Watcher** when the given condition is met. We can set any condition, such as when a filed value crosses a certain threshold value, or if there is any data anomaly in the data, or if we are receiving a certain field in our data.

Let's say these are the events that are critical to us, and we should know whenever they occur. For these situations, we can configure the alerts in Kibana so that we can get a timely notification. In Kibana UI, we can configure the watch for any such condition that is generated by the Elasticsearch query in the background to keep checking the data..

When the configured condition is met, Elasticsearch triggers the alerting system action, for example, sending a notification. These actions can be to send an email, to notify through a third-party tool such as Slack, or to add a log entry or any other third-party integration. We can open the **Alert** page by clicking on the **Management** link from the left menu, and then click on the **Watcher** link under **Elasticsearch**; see the following screenshot:

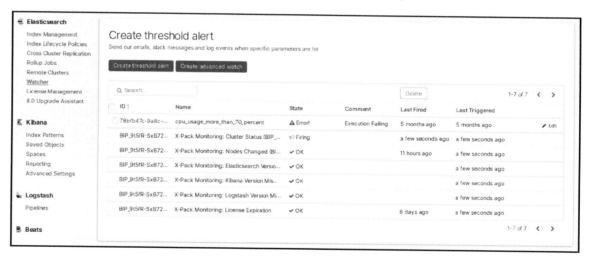

The preceding screenshot shows the **Watcher** page with a list of the existing watches; from this page, we can create threshold alerts or advanced watch. **Watcher** history is maintained in the Elasticsearch index, where we can get the complete information of a watcher. These details can include when it was executed, the results of its execution, whether the given condition was met, and what the output of the watcher was.

Creating a threshold alert

Now, let's see how a watcher can be created in Kibana to configure a threshold alert. So, we need to do the following three things to configure a watch:

1. Schedule a watch on single or multiple fields.
2. Set a condition to match.
3. Configure the action to be performed.

In the first step, we have to select the Elasticsearch index and its fields on which we want to create the watch. Then, we need to set the condition to be checked in a periodic manner, and follow this up with the action that would be performed when the given condition is met.

In Kibana, we can create a watch in the following steps:

1. On the **Watcher** listing page, click on the **Create threshold alert** button, which will open the **Create a new threshold alert** page.
2. On this page, add the name, select the indices, and set the time field. So, we are setting the name as `cpu_usage_more_than_75_percent`; and for the index, we are picking the Metricbeat index pattern; for the time field, we are picking **@timestamp** and duration is set as **10 seconds**. Please refer to the following screenshot:

The preceding screenshot shows the **Create new threshold alert** page. Under the **Matching the following condition** section, set the condition that needs checking using the interactive interface.

3. So here, we need to add the condition on the **system.process.cpu.total.pct** field of the **metricbeat*** index pattern. To set this condition, we need to set the **max()** function for **WHEN** to check, with a max value of **system.process.cpu.total.pct**, by setting this field under **OF**.

4. Then, select **all documents** for **OVER** and set **0.75** for **IS ABOVE** to check whether the maximum value of the field goes beyond **0.75**. Finally, set 1 minute, or any duration, for **FOR THE LAST** duration. See the following screenshot:

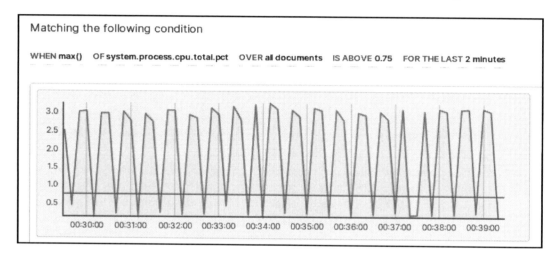

The preceding screenshot shows the condition section of the watch screen.

5. Now, set the action to be performed by selecting the action from the **Add new action** dropdown. We can send an email, log a message, or send a message to Slack using this option. So here, we can send an email to any email address, but before setting it up, we need to add the SMTP credential in the `elasticsearch.yml` file. I have configured the Gmail SMTP accounts to send emails and added the following configuration in my `elasticsearch.yml` file:

```
xpack.notification.email.account:
  gmail_account:
    profile: gmail
    smtp:
      auth: true
      starttls.enable: true
      host: smtp.gmail.com
      port: 587
      user: a******@gmail.com
      password: w*****@****
```

6. Click on the **E-mail** option from the add **New action** dropdown. Add the email address under the **To e-mail address** text box.

7. Now, edit the **Subject** section as per the requirements and add the message in the **Body** section.

8. After adding these details, click on the **Test fire an e-mail now** button to test the email flow.

9. Afterward, click on the **Save** button to save the watch; refer to the following screenshot:

The preceding screenshot shows the action block of the alerting page. This way, we can create the condition and, using the email action, can notify to the provided email ID once the condition is met.

Reporting

Reporting is again a very useful Elastic Stack feature, as using this we can generate CSV, PDF, or PNG reports from the Kibana discover, dashboards, or visualizations view. The same reports can be downloaded by clicking on the **Reporting** link under **Kibana** on the **Management** page. This will open the **Reporting** page, and with a listing of all generated reports and from this list, we can download the desired report; refer to the following screenshot:

Reports

Find reports generated in Kibana applications here

Report	Created at	Status	Actions
metricbeat_discover search	2019-05-20 @ 01:14 AM elastic	Completed at 2019-05-20 @ 01:14 AM	⊕ ⓘ
apache_http_response dashboard	2018-12-30 @ 05:04 PM elastic	Completed at 2018-12-30 @ 05:04 PM	⊕ ⓘ
apache_response_code-donut visualization	2018-12-30 @ 05:03 PM elastic	Completed at 2018-12-30 @ 05:03 PM	⊕ ⓘ
ML Apache2 Access Data search	2018-12-30 @ 04:59 PM elastic	Completed at 2018-12-30 @ 04:59 PM	⊕ ⓘ
ML Apache2 Access Data search	2018-12-30 @ 04:56 PM elastic	Completed at 2018-12-30 @ 04:56 PM	⊕ ⓘ
apache_http_response dashboard	2018-12-22 @ 11:35 PM elastic	Completed at 2018-12-22 @ 11:35 PM	⊕ ⓘ

The preceding screenshot shows all the reports that we have generated from different places, such as the search, visualization, or dashboard page. This is the **Reporting** page, from where we can download the reports, but now we will cover the places from where we can generate these reports.

CSV reports

CSV reports are quite handy sometimes, as we are very much familiar with the spreadsheet software and can play around with CSV data. From Kibana discover, we can perform search and filter operations and, after applying those on the index pattern, we can generate the reports. Although the reports can be generated without any search or filter, it may be useful to get the report with certain search or filter criteria.

We can generate the CSV report from the Kibana discover page in the following steps:

1. Apply the search and filter on the **Discover** page of Kibana and save it by providing the name for the saved object.
2. Click on the **Share** link on the top left; this will open a pop-up box, as shown in the following screenshot:

3. Now, click on the **CSV Report** link, which will open the **CSV Reports** popup, as shown in the following screenshot:

4. Now, click on the **Generate CSV** button, which will generate the CSV report. On the screen, we can see the success message on the bottom-right corner of the page. This success message has the **Download report** button, through which we can download the report. The same report can also be downloaded from the **Reporting** page on the **Management** page of **Kibana**.

PDF and PNG reports

From the saved **Dashboard** or **Visualization** screen, we can download the report in the form of PDF or PNG. The option to generate the reports from **Dashboard** and **Visualization** is very similar, so we are going to take the example of **Dashboard** to explain the PDF or PNG report download. To download the PDF or PNG report from a **Dashboard**, we need to do the following:

1. Click on the **Share** link in the top-left of the page. This will open the popup with multiple links.
2. From the popup, click on **PDF Reports** to generate the PDF report or **PNG Report** to download the PNG report; see the following screenshot:

3. This will open the popup with the **Generate PDF** or **Generate PNG** button; see the following screenshot:

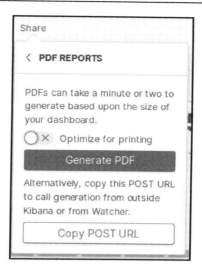

4. Now, click on the **Generate PDF** or **Generate PNG** button to generate the report. This will generate the PDF or PNG report.

This way, we can generate the reports in CSV, PDF, or PNG format using the reporting feature of Kibana. These reports are handy and can easily be shared with anyone.

Summary

In this chapter, we have discussed Elastic Stack features and why they are important. We have started with an introduction, and then moved on to the security feature. Under security, we have covered user and role management, and explained it in a practical way by creating a role and a user, and then by assigning the role to the user. Then, we covered monitoring; we saw how to monitor the Elastic Stack using this feature.

We covered Elasticsearch and Kibana monitoring with different metrics in the form of a summary and graphs. After monitoring, we covered the alerting system and explained how to create a threshold alert in a practical way by taking the example of metricbeat data. Lastly, we explained how to generate CSV, PDF, or PNG reports from the Kibana Discover, Visualize, or Dashboard page. We have explained all the important features of Elastic Stack in this chapter.

In the next chapter, we will cover the Kibana Canvas and Plugins. Using Canvas, we can express our creativity to create visualizations, while through plugins we can extend the features of Kibana.

Kibana Canvas and Plugins

8

In this chapter, we are going to discuss Kibana Canvas, which is a great feature of Kibana as it allows us to create our design and display the data on it. Using Canvas, we can make our data look amazing as we can create pixel-perfect designs through it. We can also show our data by using our own text, color, and shapes, and can also present our own creativity to create the visualizations.

It provides us a fresh new way to visualize our data, unlike the traditional Kibana Visualize. In this chapter, we will learn how to generate Canvas visualizations. After Canvas, we will explain how to use the Kibana plugins to generate our own plugin. We can enable add-on functionality in Kibana using Kibana plugins. This is still in the state of constant development. In this chapter, we are going to cover the following:

- Introduction to Canvas
- Adding elements in Canvas
- Adding a data table, pie chart, and static image in Canvas
- Creating a presentation in Canvas
- Installing and removing Kibana plugins

Kibana Canvas

Kibana provides us a way to show our creativity for showing data in a visual form. Previously, we were using Kibana Visualize to create different types of visualizations such as a bar chart, line chart, tag cloud, data table, heatmap, and more. But Canvas is more than that, as we can create these visualizations along with other customization options. Using Canvas, we can play around with custom texts, different colors, shapes, and images. It helps us to group different types of visualizations on a single page. As we have already covered how to create different visualizations in Kibana Visualize, let's now jump into Canvas, and create a few visualizations such as a data table and pie chart to understand more about Kibana Canvas.

Introduction to Canvas

Here, we will see how we can start with Kibana Canvas by adding different elements on the **Canvas** workpad. So, to start with, we need to click on the **Canvas** link from the left menu of Kibana, which will open the **Canvas** screen of Kibana with different options; please refer to the following screenshot:

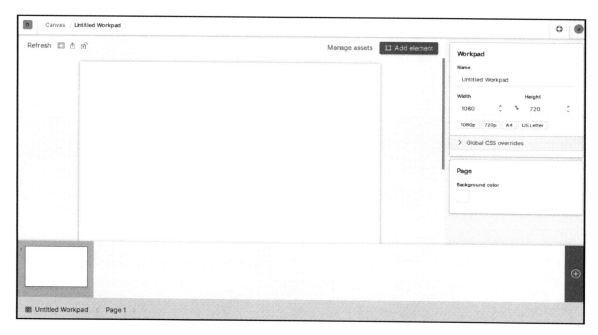

The preceding screenshot shows the default page of Kibana Canvas. Here, we can see some links above the workpad; the left **Refresh** link is there to set the page refresh, and here we set the auto-refresh interval or can click on the **Refresh** button to refresh the page manually. Please refer to the following screenshot:

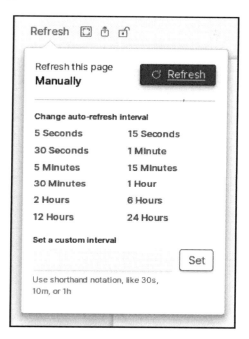

The preceding screenshot shows the refresh pop-up view, from where we can pick any time interval for an auto-refresh. We have a **Set** button, using which we can set the custom interval, and a **Refresh** button, using which we can manually refresh the workpad. After the **Refresh** link, we have a fullscreen icon to toggle the workpad in fullscreen and normal mode. After the fullscreen icon, the third icon is there to share the workpad, using which we can download the workpad in the form of JSON or PDF. Please refer to the following screenshot:

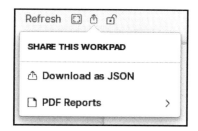

The preceding screenshot shows the share popup, where we can see two links, **Download as JSON** and **PDF Reports**, for downloading the Canvas workpad. The fourth icon is there to show or hide the editing controls. It is good to expand the workpad when editing is not required and we want to show it to someone.

Customizing the workpad

We can customize the **Workpad** page by modifying it from the right-hand pane. It has different options such as the Canvas workpad file **Name**, which we can change from there. Then, we have the **Width** and **Height** of the workpad, which we can adjust as per our requirements. We also have links for some custom sizes such as **1080p**, **720p**, **A4**, and **US Letter**.

We can also override the global CSS using the **Global CSS overrides** option. At last, we have a **Background color** option under **Page** that we can change to change the workpad background color; please refer to the following screenshot:

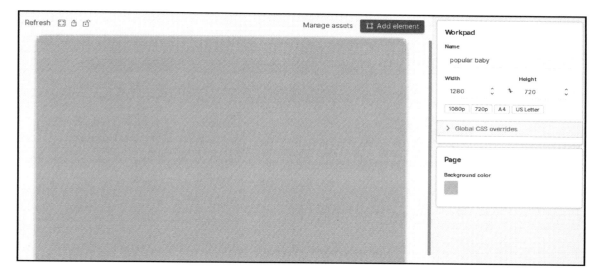

In the preceding screenshot, we can see that we have changed the background color to light green and changed the workpad size to **720p**. This way, we can customize the Canvas workpad.

Managing assets

Managing assets is a nice way to store all the assets in a central place, from where we can add them to the workpad whenever we need to add the desired asset. Here, we can import any image file and can delete it from the workpad asset. The following screenshot shows the **Manage workpad assets** screen of Kibana Canvas:

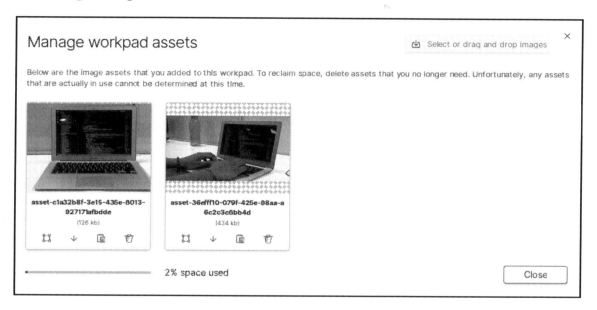

The preceding screenshot shows the **Manage workpad assets** pop-up screen, using which we can upload any image. It is a kind of image library for Kibana Canvas, using which we can easily use any image asset for designing the Canvas visualization. In this popup, we have a **Select or drag and drop images** button, using which we can import any image or drag and drop the image. There are four links below each image, using which we can perform different operations; please refer to the following screenshot:

In the preceding screenshot, we can see the single image from the **Manage workpad assets** view. It basically shows the image thumbnail and the asset name and its size; after the image size, it shows four links. The first link is there to create the image element in the Canvas workpad, the second link is there to download the image, the third link is to copy the image to the clipboard, and the last link is there to delete the image from **Managed workpad assets**.

Using these links, we can manage different images on the Kibana Canvas **Manage workpad assets** screen. Following the images, we have a progress bar along with a message that shows **x% space used**, where *x* is showing the total space that is used by the asset images.

Adding elements

On the Canvas workpad, we can add different elements using the different options that are available. If we want to add any element on the Canvas workpad, then we need to click on the **Add element** button, which will open the following screen:

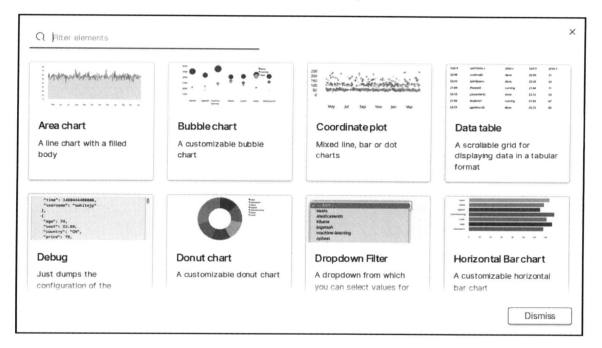

The preceding screenshot shows the add element screen, from where we can insert different types of visualizations. These elements can be of the following types:

- **Area chart**
- **Bubble chart**
- **Coordinate plot**
- **Data table**
- **Debug**
- **Donut chart**
- **Dropdown Filter**

- **Horizontal Bar chart**
- **Horizontal Progress bar**
- **Horizontal Progress pill**
- **Static image**
- **Image repeat**
- **Image reveal**
- **Line chart**
- **Markdown**
- **Metric**
- **Pie chart**
- **Progress gauge**
- **Progress semicircle**
- **Progress wheel**
- **Shape**
- **Tilted Pie chart**
- **Time filter**
- **Vertical Progress bar**
- **Vertical Progress pill**
- **Vertical Bar chart**

From the pop-up screen, we can insert any visualization element on the Canvas workpad, as per the requirements. If we don't want to add any visualization, then we can click on the **Dismiss** button in the bottom-right of the screen. There are too many elements that we can use under Kibana Canvas, but it is not possible to cover each and every element type in this book, and that is why we are going to cover some important types of visualization.

Data tables

We have already covered data tables under Kibana Visualization, where we have covered how to display the Elasticsearch index data in a tabular way. In Kibana Canvas, we can also add data tables, but here we have more control over the presentation part of it. Here, we can apply custom CSS on the table classes and can change the design, apply a custom background, and more.

To add a data table in Kibana Canvas, we need to do the following:

1. Click on the **Add element** button in the top-right corner above the Canvas workpad. This will open the element type selection pop-up screen.
2. Click on the **Data table** block from the pop-up screen. This will add the data table in the Canvas workpad; see the following screenshot:

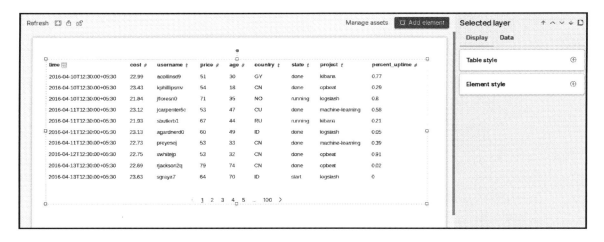

3. Now, select the data table on the workpad, which will enable the right pane for the **Selected layer**.

4. Click on the **Data** link to open the tab for changing the data source. See the following screenshot:

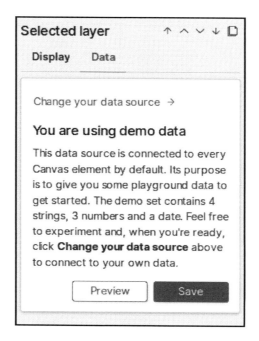

5. Now, click on the **Change your data source** link, which will open the data source selection screen with four options: **Timelion**, **Demo data**, **Elasticseach SQL**, and **Elasticsearch raw documents**. See the following screenshot:

6. Now, click on the **Elasticsearch raw documents** option, which will open the **Change your data source** screen with the option to change **Index**, **Query**, **Sort Field**, **Sort Order**, and **Fields**. Here, we will use the **popular-baby-names** index, which we have already covered earlier.

7. In the **Fields** column, we can add the `Child's First Name`, `Ethnicity`, `Year of Birth`, `Rank`, and `Count` fields. The following screenshot shows the index selection pane:

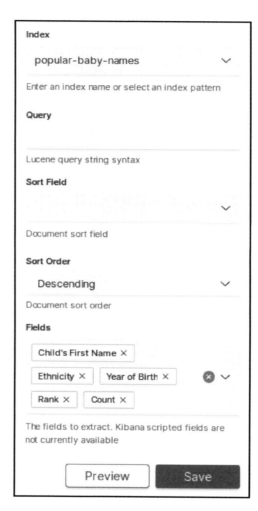

8. After adding the index and fields, we can click on the **Preview** button to see a preview of the data.

9. After verifying the preview, we can click on the **Save** button to save the data source. This will change the data table view as per the newly saved data source; please refer to the following screenshot:

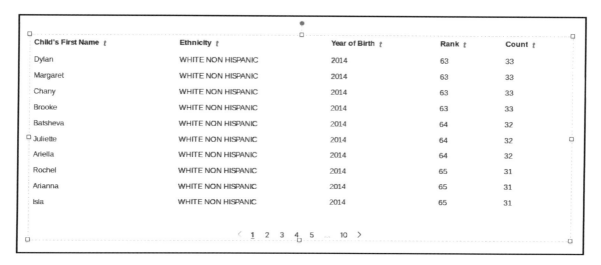

Child's First Name	Ethnicity	Year of Birth	Rank	Count
Dylan	WHITE NON HISPANIC	2014	63	33
Margaret	WHITE NON HISPANIC	2014	63	33
Chany	WHITE NON HISPANIC	2014	63	33
Brooke	WHITE NON HISPANIC	2014	63	33
Batsheva	WHITE NON HISPANIC	2014	64	32
Juliette	WHITE NON HISPANIC	2014	64	32
Ariella	WHITE NON HISPANIC	2014	64	32
Rochel	WHITE NON HISPANIC	2014	65	31
Arianna	WHITE NON HISPANIC	2014	65	31
Isla	WHITE NON HISPANIC	2014	65	31

‹ 1 2 3 4 5 ... 10 ›

The preceding screenshot shows the data from the **popular-baby-names** index with the selected columns. This way, we can show tabular data from any index on the Kibana Canvas workpad using data tables.

Designing the data table

As we have added the data table on the workpad, let's design it to make it more attractive. Under table designing, we will cover how to change the text color, font, size, and more, and then we will see how to apply custom CSS classes to the data table. To play with the table style, we need to do the following:

1. From the right-side **Selected layer** options, click on the **Display** link to open the display tab. It shows two options: **Table style** and **Element style**.
2. Click on the plus icon next to **Table style**, which opens a popup with multiple options such as **Text settings**, **Rows per page**, **Pagination**, and **Header**.

3. Click on the **Text settings** option to set the colors, size, and font of the text. Here, I am going to change the font, color, size, and make the text bold; see the following screenshot:

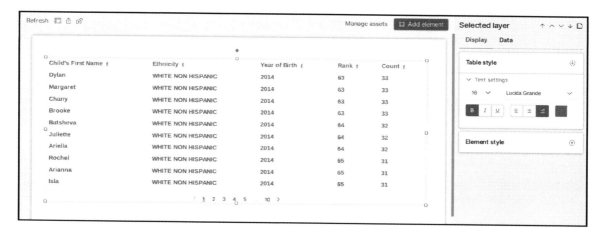

4. Now, click again on the plus icon next to **Table style**, and click on the **Rows per page** option. By default, it is set to **10**, so we can change it to **25**.

5. We can enable or disable the pagination option by clicking on the **Pagination** option from the **Table style** menu.

6. In the same way, we can enable or disable the header by clicking on the **Header** option from the **Table style** menu.

So, this way, we can customize the text of the data table by changing the font, text size, color, and more, adjust the rows per page, and show or hide the table **Header** and **Pagination** options. Now, let's explore how we can change the element style by applying custom CSS and how to change the appearance of the element container. So, to change the element style, we need to do the following:

1. Click on the plus icon next to the **Element style** text; this will open a pop-up screen with two links, **Container style** and **CSS**.

2. Click on the **Container style** link to open the container style view. Here, we can see the **APPEARANCE** and **BORDER** options.

3. Under **APPEARANCE**, we can change the **Padding, Opacity**, and **Overflow**.
4. Under the **BORDER** option, we can modify the border **Thickness, Style, Radius**, and **Color**; please refer to the following screenshot:

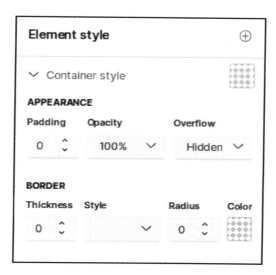

The preceding screenshot shows the **Container style** view, with the **APPEARANCE** and **BORDER** options. We can change these values to modify the data table container design:

1. Now, click on the CSS option under **Element style**; this will open the **CSS** view.
2. It opens the text area to write the CSS code and a button, **Apply stylesheet**, to apply the CSS.
3. We can modify the data table design by applying the following CSS classes for even and odd rows:

```
.canvasDataTable__tbody>:nth-child(even) {
background-color: #45bdb0;
}

.canvasDataTable__tbody>:nth-child(odd) {
background-color: #f5cc5d;
}
```

4. After pasting the preceding CSS code, we can click on **Apply stylesheet**, which will change the data table design; please refer to the following screenshot:

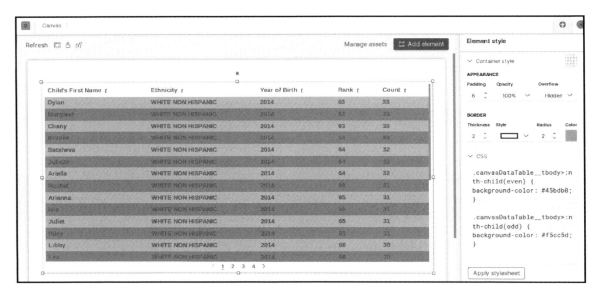

The preceding screenshot shows the data table after customizing it through the container style and CSS. Here, we can see different colors for even and odd rows of the table and a different color for the text. This way, we can customize the data table design by applying the CSS classes.

Pie charts

We have already covered the pie chart in `Chapter 4`, *Visualizing Data Using Kibana*. The pie chart is there to show the proportion of each item in the complete set of items. Here, we are going to create the pie chart using the Elasticsearch index of the crime dataset, which is taken from the US government website, `https://catalog.data.gov/dataset/crimes-2001-to-present-398a4`. This dataset has `ID`, `Date`, `Case Number`, `Primary Type`, `Block`, `IUCR`, `Description`, `Location`, `Arrest`, `Domestic`, `Beat`, `District`, `Ward`, `Community Area`, `FBI Code`, `X Coordinate`, `Y Coordinate`, `Year`, `Latitude`, `Longitude`, `Updated On`, and `Location` fields. Here, we want to see the proportion of the primary type of the crime.

I have already explained the steps to create the Elasticsearch index using CSV data in the previous chapter, so if you want to create the index for the crime dataset, then follow the steps.

So, to create the pie chart on Kibana Canvas for crime data, we need to do the following:

1. Click on the **Add element** button in the top-right corner of the page, above the workpad.
2. From the pop-up screen, click on the **Pie chart** block. This will insert a pie chart on the workpad of Canvas.
3. Select the pie chart and click on the **Data** tab from the right-hand pane.
4. Click on the **Change your data source** link; this will open a view with four different options.
5. Click on the **Elasticsearch raw documents** block; this will open a page to select the **Index**, **Sort Fields**, **Sort Order**, **Fields**, and more.
    1. Select the **crime*** index pattern to select the crime data, and click on the **Save** button.
6. Now, click on the **Display** tab from the top-right pane.
7. Under **Slice Labels**, select **Value** in the first dropdown and select **Primary Type** in the next dropdown; please refer to the following screenshot:

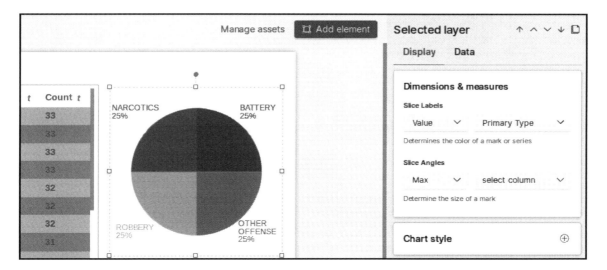

The preceding screenshot shows the pie chart with four primary crime types. Here, they are all showing 25%, which may not be the correct statistics because I have taken only a few records from the complete dataset of the US government for my Elasticsearch index. This way, we can create the pie chart in Kibana Canvas.

After adding the pie chart, we can customize it by changing the **Chart style**. Under **Chart style**, we have a lot of options such as **Inner radius**, **Labels**, **Color palette**, **Label radius**, **Legend position**, **Radius**, **Series style**, **Text settings**, and **Tilt angles**. So, to change the chart style, we need to do the following:

1. Click on the plus icon next to **Chart style**, which will open the popup with different options.
2. Click on the **Color palette** option, which provides us the option to pick the color palette for the pie chart.
3. The next option is **Inner radius**, using which we can convert the pie chart into a donut chart.
4. Then, we have the **Labels** option, using which we can enable or disable the label display on the pie chart.
5. Using the **Label radius** option, we can arrange the label location.
6. The **Legend position** option is there to set the legend position or make it hide.
7. Using the **Radius** option, we can set the radius of the pie chart.
8. The **Series style** option is there, using which we can set the color of individual fields in the pie chart.
9. Using the **Text settings** option, we can change the font, text size, color, and indentation of the pie chart.
10. And, lastly, we have a **Tilt angle**, using which we can tilt the pie chart.

See the following screenshot, where we have applied the chart style to our pie chart:

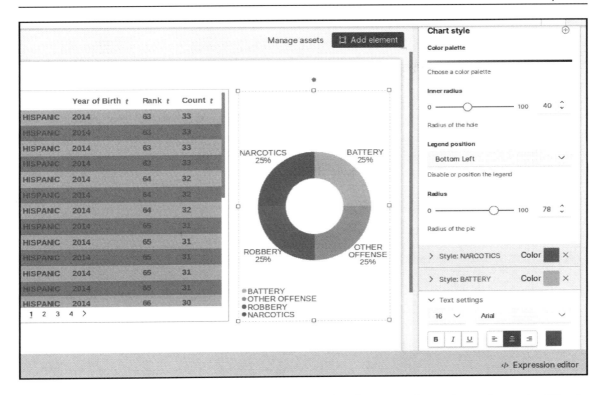

This way, using **Chart style**, we can change the style of our pie chart. Apart from the **Chart style**, we have one more option, **Element style**, where we have two options, which are **Container style** and **CSS**. We can apply the **Element style** in the following ways:

1. Click on the **Container style** from the pop-up screen, which comes after clicking on the plus icon next to **Element style**.
2. Under **Container style**, we can set the appearance through **Padding**, **Opacity**, **Overview**, and **Border** by providing the **Thickness**, border **Style**, **Radius**, and border **Color**.
3. Then, we have the **CSS** option, where we can provide the custom CSS code.

This way, we can create the pie chart and can apply styles in Kibana Canvas. It provides a wide range of customization options, which are very useful for creating attractive visualizations.

Images

We can add static images using the **Image** element type in Canvas. To add the static image on the Canvas workpad, we need to do the following:

1. From the element type pop-up screen, click on the **Image** block; this will put the Elastic logo on the workpad.
2. From the right-side **Image** options, we can pick the **Asset**, **Import**, or **Link** option to add the image. We can select the image from the **Asset** option if we have already added the image there. Using the **Import** option, we can upload an image, while using the **Link** option, we can provide the image URL.
3. As we have already added the images under **Asset**, we will click on the image thumbnail under **Asset** to add it on the workpad.
4. We can use the image in the Canvas workpad background by opening the **Container style** under **Element style** to decrease the opacity percentage. We can set it to **30%** so that we can easily see the other elements on the workpad.
5. After selecting the image, we can click on the **Move element down one layer** icon next to the **Selected layer** text in the top-right corner; please refer to the following screenshot:

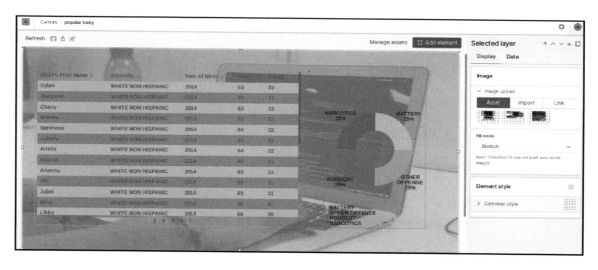

The preceding screenshot shows the Kibana Canvas workpad with a data table, a pie chart, and a static image. The static image is set in the background with an **Opacity** of **30%**. This way, we can add any static image on the Canvas workpad.

Creating a presentation in Canvas

Using Kibana Canvas, we can create a presentation that is quite different from a PowerPoint presentation, as here we can show the live data that keeps on changing. Let's assume that we need to present this workpad that we have just created. So, here, we can create an introductory workpad before the actual workpad with a data table and pie chart. We need to do the following to create a presentation using Kibana Canvas:

1. Click on the **Page 1** link in the bottom-left side of the page; this will open the workpad page view. Please refer to the following screenshot:

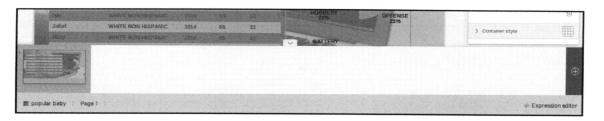

   The preceding screenshot shows the current workpad with a plus icon on the right side.

2. Now, click on the plus icon to add a new page on this workpad; this will open the new page on the current workpad.

3. We can use this page for the introduction and that is why we can drag and drop it before the existing page.

4. Now, click on **Add element** to add a **Markdown** for adding the custom text on the page. Here, I am adding the overview about the main page data visualization.

5. We can add more pages and configure them to display different data visualizations if it is required for the presentation.

6. Once we are done with the presentation, click on the full screen icon in the top-left corner of the page. This will open the first page of the workpad, as shown in the screenshot:

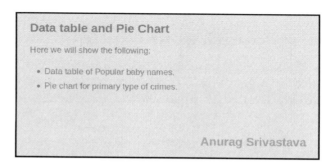

The preceding screenshot shows the introduction page of the presentation. Here, we can set the presentation introduction along with the presenter name. We can use the keyboard's left and right keys to move to the next or last page. After showing this page, we can click on the right arrow key of the keyboard, which will display the following screenshot:

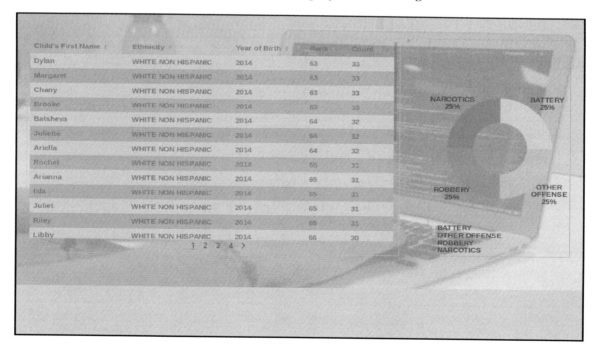

This way, we can create a dynamic presentation in Kibana Canvas. If we want to show something with our data, then it is good to create a presentation in Kibana Canvas as this always shows the visualization with the most recent data.

Kibana plugins

We can extend the Kibana core functionality by adding plugin modules. To manage the plugins, we can use the /bin/kibana-plugin command. We can search for the Kibana plugins that are compatible with the installed version of Kibana, as Kibana does not support backward compatibility for the plugins. Now, let's see how we can install a plugin in Kibana.

Installing plugins

We need to move in the Kibana home directory, as we need to run the /bin/kibana-plugin command to install the plugins. If we know the name or URL of the plugin that is compatible with the installed version of Kibana, then we can install it using the following command:

```
bin/kibana-plugin install <plugin name or URL>
```

When we provide the URL, Kibana downloads the plugin from that URL, but when we provide the name, the Kibana plugin tool tries to download it from the official Elastic plugin directory; for example, the x-pack plugin, which is an official Elastic plugin, so we can install it using the following command:

```
bin/kibana-plugin install x-pack
```

This way, we can install any compatible plugin to extend the features of Kibana. To update the plugin, we need to remove and uninstall it again. Now, let's see how we can remove the plugin.

Removing plugins

We can remove the plugin by passing the remove keyword with the plugin name to the bin/kibana-plugin command. For example, if we want to remove the x-pack plugin, then we can execute the following command:

```
bin/kibana-plugin remove x-pack
```

We can also remove the plugin manually by deleting the plugin's subdirectory from the `plugins/` directory.

Available plugins

Kibana has some known plugins that we can install in Kibana; however, for that, we first need to ensure that the plugin version is compatible with the installed Kibana version. There are many plugins such as `LogTrail`, using which we can view, search, analyze, or tail log events in real time. `Conveyor` is another plugin, using which we can import data into Elasticsearch.

Using the `Indices View` plugin, we can view the information that is related to Elasticsearch's indices. The `ElastAlert Kibana Plugin` plugin provides us a UI, using which we can create, test, and edit `ElastAlert` rules. We can see the complete list of known plugins at `https://www.elastic.co/guide/en/kibana/current/known-plugins.html`. So, after exploring a plugin's features and compatibility, we can install it in Kibana and use the features of the plugin.

Summary

In this chapter, we covered Kibana Canvas, using which we showed our creativity in visualizing data, and learned about Kibana's plugins, using which we can extend the Kibana features. We started with an introduction to Canvas, where we covered the importance of Canvas and how to customize it. Then, we covered how to manage the assets by uploading images for further use.

Then, we learned how to add different elements in Canvas, where we covered how to create a data table, and then design it. After the data table, we covered the pie chart and static images, and learned how to practically add them in a Canvas workpad. At last, we created a presentation using Canvas, and explained how this can be used to show dynamic data during a presentation.

After Canvas, we covered Kibana plugins, where we covered the installation and removal of plugins. We also discussed available Kibana plugins, so that we can check them and install the plugins as per our requirements.

In the next chapter, we will cover APM, and will explain how, using APM, we can get a complete idea about our application's performance.

9
Application Performance Monitoring

Application Performance Monitoring (APM) is built on top of the Elastic Stack. By using APM, we can monitor the performance of an application. APM is useful for the real-time monitoring of application and software services. It is quite simple to configure, as we just need to set up the APM agent for the application that we are using. Currently, the Elastic Stack supports APM agents for Java, Python's Django and Flask frameworks, RUM-JS, Node.js, Go, Ruby on Rails, Rack, and more. Once the APM agent is configured, it will collect various application-related information, such as HTTP requests, the response time for various requests, and database queries, and send this information to the APM Server. It also collects unhandled exceptions and errors; this is quite important information and using this, we can stabilize the application further.

The default search provides us with a great way to drill down even further and get additional details. So, in this chapter, we will explore what APM is, learn how to configure it, and start monitoring the application in real time. APM helps us to establish a full-stack monitoring system similar to Elastic Stack, where we can push the system logs, application logs, and database audit data into Elasticsearch. This way, after configuring the APM, we can access the end-to-end monitoring data that can show the complete details we need on a single dashboard. In this way, if something does go wrong, we can access the details of the issue by filtering through the time filter. So here, we will cover APM configuration using APM agents for Python's Django framework.

In this chapter, we will cover the following topics:

- Configuring APM agents with an application to send data to the APM Server
- Introducing the APM Server
- Installing and running the APM Server
- Configuring predefined dashboards in APM
- Elasticsearch compatibility with an APM setup
- Kibana's contribution to an APM setup
- A practical use case of APM

APM components

APM consists of four main components that work together to monitor an application. These four components are as follows:

- APM agents
- The APM Server
- Elasticsearch
- Kibana

An APM agent can be configured as an agent for any application that is supported through the Elastic APM agent. Once the agent is configured, it can capture the application data and metrics and send it to the APM Server. The APM Server then sends this data to a central Elasticsearch cluster for storage. Once the data is stored in Elasticsearch, we can view, search, and analyze it in the Kibana APM UI or on the dashboard. Take a look at the following screenshot to understand more about the architecture of these APM components:

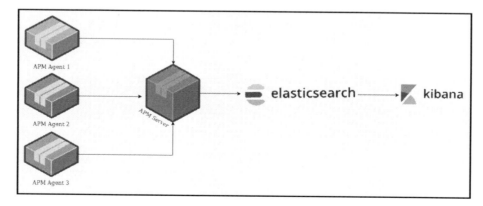

The preceding screenshot shows the architecture of APM's components. Here, we have three APM agents that are connected to an APM Server and are sending application metrics and data to the APM Server. The APM Server is pushing the data to an Elasticsearch cluster from where Kibana collects this data to show it in the Kibana APM UI or a dashboard. Then, from the Kibana interface, we can view, search, and analyze the data. In this way, we can set up the APM components for monitoring application performance. Now, let's discuss each of the APM components in detail, starting with APM agents.

APM agents

Elastic APM agents are open source libraries that can be configured in supported languages and frameworks. They are built in the same native language that they support and that is why it is quite easy to configure them. In this book, I will take the example of an APM agent for Python Django that is written in Python and can easily be configured with Python's Django framework. APM agents can be installed as a library in the same way that we install other libraries in any application. Once the APM agent is configured, it can be used to collect data, metrics, errors, and more from the application at runtime. The APM agent can buffer the data for a period of time and then send it to the APM Server. The APM Server sends this data to the Elasticsearch cluster, where it is stored for further analysis. Kibana fetches this APM data from Elasticsearch and displays the metrics through a dedicated APM UI, or through the dashboard after configuring it with the APM data.

Elastic has a dedicated APM team that is working to bring more and more APM agents to support a wide range of application languages and frameworks. We have the support of Java, Go, Python, RUM-JS, Ruby on Rails, Rack, and more through the official Elastic APM library. Apart from official agents, we can also get a lot of other agents that can be configured to send metrics and data to the APM Server. We can configure APM by checking the APM setup instructions after clicking on the **Setup Instructions** button on the **APM** page in **Kibana**.

This setup page lists the instructions to configure the APM Server and agents, as shown in the following screenshot:

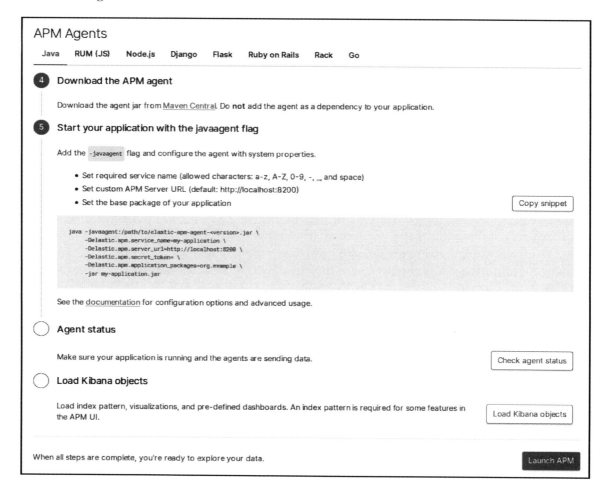

At the top, we can see the instructions to configure the APM agents in various supported languages and frameworks such as **Java, RUM (JS), Node.js, Django, Flask, Ruby on Rails, Rack**, and **Go**. Underneath the configuration section, we can see the **Agent status**, from where we can check whether the agent is configured properly or not. Finally, we have the **Load Kibana objects** option that we can use to load index patterns, visualizations, and predefined dashboards. Once everything is configured properly, we can click on the **Launch APM** button to launch the **APM** page. In this way, we can configure and set up the APM agent from a single instruction page, and start getting data and metrics from the application.

The APM Server

The APM Server is freely available with Elastic Stack and there is no need to purchase a license in order to set it up. It is written in the Go language and receives data from different APM agents that we can configure with the application. It listens to the default port, 8200, and receives data in the form of JSON through the HTTP API. After receiving data from different agents, the APM Server groups them to create the documents that Elasticsearch can index, and then sends them to Elasticsearch. Elastic Stack uses the Beats framework in the background to create the APM Server and utilizes Beats' functionalities.

The APM Server is a separate component that is usually installed on a dedicated machine. It sits between the APM agents and Elasticsearch, and converts the data that it receives from the APM agents before sending it to Elasticsearch. Note that the APM Server can easily be scaled, so we can scale APM Server as per our requirements. This avoids a security risk because it handles the data from the APM agents directly and avoids Elasticsearch being exposed in the browser. It also controls the amount of data we are sending to Elasticsearch and can buffer the data in case Elasticsearch goes down. We have different types of agents based on different languages and frameworks. These are used to send different types of data, so it is the work of the APM Server to unify the format before sending it to Elasticsearch. We can open the APM Server installation and configuration instructions by clicking on the **Setup Instructions** button on the **APM** page.

The following link has a screenshot which displays a detailed view of APM Server configuration section on the APM setup page: https://github.com/PacktPublishing/Learning-Kibana-7-Second-Edition/tree/master/Images

The screenshot details the installation steps for the APM Server on different environments such as **macOS, DEB, RPM**, and **Windows**. It also provides instructions on how to start the APM Server and how to check the status of the server. By using a single **Setup Instructions** page, we can install and configure the APM Server and APM agents. Now we will check the installation process of the APM Server on different operating systems.

Installing the APM Server

We first need to download the APM Server from Elastic's APM download page (`https://www.elastic.co/downloads/apm`) depending on the operating system we are using. Once the APM Server is downloaded, we can install it using the repositories from YUM or APT, and it can be installed as a service on the Windows machine. Now, let's understand the installation process for these different operating systems.

APT

We can install the APM Server with the APT repository using the following steps:

1. First, we need to download the public signing key and then install it:

   ```
   wget -qO - https://artifacts.elastic.co/GPG-KEY-elasticsearch |
   sudo apt-key add -
   ```

2. Then, we have to install the `apt-transport-https` package on Debian using the following command:

   ```
   sudo apt-get install apt-transport-https
   ```

3. After that, we need to save the repository definition to `/etc/apt/sources.list.d/elastic-7.x.list` using the following command:

   ```
   echo "deb https://artifacts.elastic.co/packages/7.x/apt stable
   main" | sudo tee -a /etc/apt/sources.list.d/elastic-7.x.list
   ```

4. After adding the repository definition, we need to run `apt-get update`, and then we can install the APM Server by executing the following command:

   ```
   sudo apt-get update && sudo apt-get install apm-server
   ```

5. In this way, we can install the APM Server. Now, to configure it to start automatically after every boot, we need to execute the following command:

```
sudo update-rc.d apm-server defaults 95 10
```

So, in this way, we can install and configure the APM Server using the APT repositories. Now, we are going to demonstrate the installation of the APM Server using the YUM repositories.

YUM

To install the APM Server using the YUM repository, we need to perform the following steps:

1. First, we need to download the public signing key and then install it.sudo:

```
rpm --import https://packages.elastic.co/GPG-KEY-elasticsearch
```

2. Then, we have to create an elastic repo file using the .repo extension. Let's create the elastic.repo file inside the /etc/yum.repos.d/ directory, and add the following content:

```
[elastic-7.x]
name=Elastic repository for 7.x packages
baseurl=https://artifacts.elastic.co/packages/7.x/yum
gpgcheck=1
gpgkey=https://artifacts.elastic.co/GPG-KEY-elasticsearch
enabled=1
autorefresh=1
type=rpm-md
```

3. After adding the preceding lines in the elastic.repo file, our repository is ready and we can install the APM Server using the following command:

```
yum install apm-server
```

4. To configure the APM Server to start automatically after every boot, we need to execute the following command:

```
sudo chkconfig --add apm-server
```

So, in this way, we can install and configure the APM Server using the YUM repositories.

APM Server installation on Windows

To install the APM Server on Windows, we need to perform the following steps:

1. First, download the Windows ZIP from the APM download page of Elastic (https://www.elastic.co/downloads/apm).

2. Once the ZIP is downloaded, we can extract the contents into `C:\Program Files`.

3. Now we need to rename extracted directory name from `apm-server-<version>-windows` to the `APM-Server` directory.

4. Open PowerShell using the admin rights, and then run the following command:

```
PS > cd 'C:\Program Files\APM-Server'
PS C:\Program Files\APM-Server> .\install-service-apm-server.ps1
```

5. After successfully executing the preceding command, we can install the APM Server on a Windows machine.

Running the APM Server

Once the APM Server is installed on the system, we need to start it so that we can begin getting data from the APM agents. To start the APM Server, we need to run the following command:

```
./apm-server -e
```

Using the `-e` global flag, we can enable the logging to `stderr` and disable `syslog` or the file output.

Configuring the APM Server

We can configure the APM Server using the `apm-server.yml` configuration file. Using this file, we can change the Elasticsearch endpoint (or its credentials), which is where the APM Server is going to send the data, host, and the ports. The following code snippet shows an example of the `config` file data:

```
apm-server:
  host: "localhost:8200"
  rum:
    enabled: true
queue.mem.events: 4096
max_procs: 4
```

There are different options that we can modify from the APM Server configuration file, such as `host`, `max_header_size`, `read_timeout`, `write_timeout`, `shutdown_timeout`, `max_event_size`, `max_connection`, `secret_token`, `flush.timeout`, and more. We can configure the Elasticseach output by providing `hosts`, `username`, and `password`, as shown in the following expression:

```
output.elasticsearch:
  hosts: ["https://localhost:9200"]
  username: "apm-server_internal"
  password: "YOUR_PASSWORD"
```

In the preceding expression, we have provided the Elasticsearch host address, the username, and the password using the APM Server, which will connect and send the data to Elasticsearch. In this way, we can modify the configuration as per our requirements.

Elasticsearch

The APM Server sends metric and error data received from the APM agents to the Elasticsearch cluster. We can utilize the search and aggregation capabilities of Elasticsearch to analyze APM data. So, essentially, Elasticsearch stores all the APM data that can then be analyzed or visualized in Kibana.

Kibana

We have two options in Kibana to visualize APM data. The first option is to use the dedicated APM UI that is available under the APM link in the left-hand side menu. The second option is to use the default Kibana dashboard, which is mainly used to visualize other data sources. As we have covered how to install and configure the APM Server with Elastic Stack, we will now learn how to configure a Python Django application with APM.

Configuring an application with APM

Now, we will look at a practical example in which we are going to configure the APM agent to access the data and metrics and send them to the APM Server. So far, we have learned how to install and configure the APM agent and the APM Server. Here, we will take the example of a simple blog website that is built in the Django framework of Python. We are going to carry out the following steps:

1. Configure the APM agent for the Django application.
2. Run the Django application.
3. Monitor the APM data using the APM UI or Kibana dashboard.

From the **Setup Instructions** page, we can check the status of the APM agent and the APM Server.

The following link has a screenshot which displays the **APM Agents** instructions page: `https://github.com/PacktPublishing/Learning-Kibana-7-Second-Edition/tree/master/Images`

In the screenshot, we can see the Django configuration steps, as it shows the steps in a sequence. The first step is to **Install the APM agent**, and then **Configure the agent**. Following this, we can check the **Agent status** and, finally, we can **Load Kibana objects** to the **APM**. In this way, we can install the agent and then monitor whether everything is configured properly. Once everything is working, we click on the **Launch APM** button to launch the **APM** page.

Configuring the APM agent for the Django application

Here, we will look at an example of a Python Django application for blog creation and listing. In the next section, we will explain more about this blog application that is built in Python Django. But, first, we will cover how to configure the APM agent with this application so that we can get the application's performance data in Kibana:

1. To configure Django to run the APM agent for Python, we need to install the `elastic-apm` module:

```
pip install elastic-apm
```

2. Then, we need to configure the agent and configure APM with this Django application. We need to make the following changes in the `settings.py` file:

```
# Add the agent to the installed apps
INSTALLED_APPS = (
  'elasticapm.contrib.django',
  # ...
)

ELASTIC_APM = {
  # Set required service name. Allowed characters:
  # a-z, A-Z, 0-9, -, _, and space
  'SERVICE_NAME': 'django application',

  # Use if APM Server requires a token
  'SECRET_TOKEN': 'mysecrettoken',

  # Set custom APM Server URL (default: http://localhost:8200)
  'SERVER_URL': 'http://localhost:8200',
}

# To send performance metrics, add our tracing middleware:
MIDDLEWARE = (
  'elasticapm.contrib.django.middleware.TracingMiddleware',
  #...
)
```

Using the preceding changes in the `settings.py` file, the APM agent can be configured to the Python Django application.

3. After making these changes in the `settings.py` file, we can start the application and then verify from the **Setup Instructions** page whether everything is working as per our expectations.

Running the Django application

You can get this Django blog application from the GitHub repository for this book (`https:/ /github.com/PacktPublishing/Learning-Kibana-7-Second-Edition`). Now, we will learn more about the blog application and demonstrate how to run it:

1. We need to download this application from the GitHub page, and then navigate inside the main directory to execute the following commands:

```
# make migrations
python3 manage.py makemigrations

# migrate the tables
python3 manage.py migrate

# run the server
python3 manage.py runserver
```

2. After successfully executing the preceding command, we can run the server using the following URL:

```
http://127.0.0.1:8000/blogs
```

3. We can access `swagger` using the following link:

```
http://127.0.0.1:8000/swagger/
```

This application is very simple: the user can add blogs and list them using the API. The following screenshot shows the default UI of Django for adding a blog:

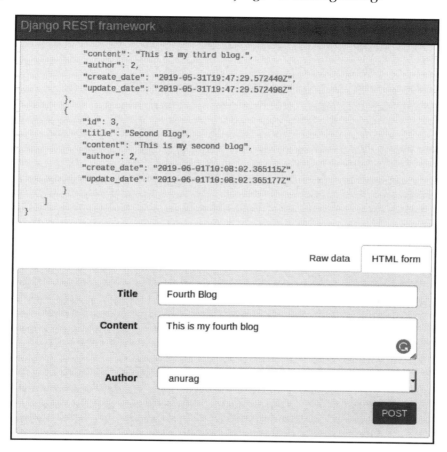

The preceding screenshot shows the Django blog application UI screen, where we can add a blog and list it. In this way, we can configure the APM agent with the Django application. Similarly, APM agents can be configured in all the supported languages and frameworks. We can verify whether the APM agent is sending the data by clicking on the **Check agent status** button on the **Setup Instructions** page.

Monitoring the APM data

Once the APM agent is configured and starts sending data, we can monitor the APM data using the APM UI or through the Kibana dashboard:

We can open the **APM** page by clicking on the **Launch APM** button from the **Setup Instructions** page; alternatively, the page can be directly opened by clicking on the **APM** link in the left-hand menu, as shown in the following screenshot:

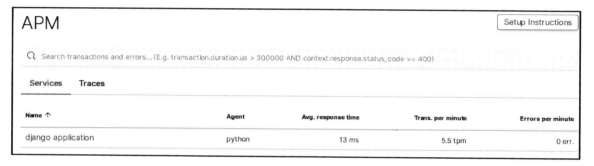

The preceding screenshot shows the APM service name, which is **django application**. This name was configured for the APM agent configuration inside the Django application. We can examine the details by clicking on the service name. A screenshot of the details can be observed in the following link: `https://github.com/PacktPublishing/Learning-Kibana-7-Second-Edition/tree/master/Images`

The screenshot shows the transaction details in the form of graphs such as **Transaction duration** and **Requests per minute**. Underneath the graphs, we can see different types of requests, such as `GET` and `POST`, along with the average duration, 95th percentile, transactions per minute, and impact. We can click on the request type links to see more details about that particular type; for example, we can see **Transaction duration distribution** and **Transaction sample**. Under the transaction sample, we can see the **Timeline**, which shows the breakup of a **request**; **Url**, which shows the URL and port details; and **HTTP**, which shows the details of **requests**, such as `cookies`, `env`, `headers`, `method`, and `socket`, and the details of **response**, including `headers` and `status code`:

Timeline	Url	HTTP	Host	Service	Process	User	Labels

request

body
```
{
    "original": "[REDACTED]"
}
```

cookies
```
{
    "csrftoken": "********",
    "tabstyle": "html-tab"
}
```

env
```
{
    "REMOTE_ADDR": "127.0.0.1",
    "SERVER_NAME": "localhost",
    "SERVER_PORT": "8000"
}
```

headers
```
{
    "accept": "text/html,application/xhtml+xml,application/xml;q=0.9,*/*;q=0.8",
    "accept-encoding": "gzip, deflate",
    "cookie": "csrftoken=********; tabstyle=html-tab",
    "connection": "keep-alive",
    "content-type": "multipart/form-data; boundary=---------------------------14811277116049643535739268045",
    "accept-language": "en-US,en;q=0.5",
    "referer": "http://127.0.0.1:8000/blogs/",
    "upgrade-insecure-requests": "1",
    "content-length": "601",
    "host": "127.0.0.1:8000",
    "user-agent": "Mozilla/5.0 (X11; Ubuntu; Linux x86_64; rv:66.0) Gecko/20100101 Firefox/66.0"
}
```

method   post

socket
```
{
    "remote_address": "127.0.0.1",
    "encrypted": false
}
```

response

headers
```
{
    "Content-Type": "text/html; charset=utf-8",
    "Vary": "Accept",
    "Allow": "GET, POST, HEAD, OPTIONS"
}
```

status_code   201

We also have the **Host** tab that displays the hostname, architecture, platform, IP, name, and OS details. Next to **Host**, we can see the **Service** details, such as the routine name and version, the framework name and version, and the language name and version. Next, we have the **Process** link that we can use to get the process ID and arguments, and then, we can see the user details using the **User** link. A screenshot showing the details page of the GET type of requests can be observed in the following link: https://github.com/PacktPublishing/Learning-Kibana-7-Second-Edition/tree/master/Images

The screenshot shows the details of the GET request, where we can see the **Transactions duration distribution** and **Transaction sample** details. We can click on the **Traces** link next to the **Services** tab to see the different types of requests, such as GET and POST; take a look at the following screenshot:

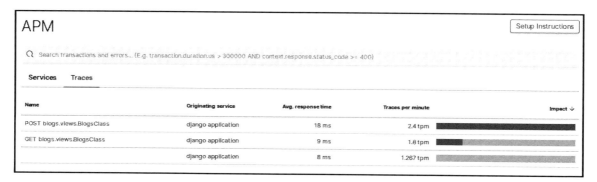

In the preceding screenshot, we can see the POST and GET requests and we can examine the details by clicking on the links. In this way, we can monitor the application and get all the details that are required to debug the application if there is an issue. By clicking on the **Load Kibana objects** button from the **Setup Instructions** page, we can import the saved objects, visualizations, dashboards, and more. Additionally, we can access them and see the application monitoring data. In this way, we can configure the monitoring for any application using the APM agent and server.

Summary

In this chapter, we covered application monitoring using Elastic APM. We started with an introduction to APM and learned how to use it to monitor the performance of an application. Then, we covered the different components of APM, such as agents, the server, Elasticsearch, and Kibana. Following this, we covered the installation and configuration of the APM Server and APM agents. Then, we explore the configuration of the APM agent with a Python Django application for blog creation and listing. After the APM agent configuration, we examined the APM UI through different metrics and graphs, which we can use to monitor the application.

In the next chapter, we will cover the machine learning features of Kibana to understand how we can detect anomalies in the data, and access future trends using the current set of data.

Machine Learning with Kibana 10

We are in the age of digital transformation, where data is growing at an accelerating pace. As data size is growing day by day, it is creating a lot of complexity as it is difficult to drill down and get meaningful information. Still, while a lot of people use the old traditional way to identify issues in their application, there are many people who are using monitoring tools to identify these issues, and this number is increasing.

Let's take a simple example where we have an issue in the application and we want to drill down to the root cause through the operational log. One way to do this is to drill down into all the related data using the same time series that was used when the probable issue occurred. Another way is to use machine learning so that we can easily find the data anomaly. So, we can say that, using machine learning, we can reduce the time and complexity for a human to manually inspect the dashboards or to create the rules, using which any issue can be captured.

In this chapter, we are going to cover the following topics:

- What is Elastic machine learning?
- Machine learning features
- Creating machine learning jobs
- Data visualizer
- Single metric jobs
- Forecasting using machine learning
- Multimetric jobs
- Population jobs

What is Elastic machine learning?

Machine learning helps us to spot any data-anomaly-related issues such as a cyber attacks, business issues, or infrastructure-related issues. Elastic machine learning uses unsupervised learning and it automatically models the normal behavior of the time series data. For creating the model, it learns the trends and periodicity in real time and, using that model, it identifies the anomalies in the data. Elastic machine learning features run through Elasticsearch, and we can initiate, monitor, and visualize the machine learning results in Kibana as it provides an intuitive UI. For machine learning features, we need to take the X-Pack license as a basic license. We can only use the data visualizer to explore the data that is stored in Elasticsearch.

Elastic machine learning works with time series data such as operational logs, Beats data, or any other application data. Machine learning jobs work by reading the normal trend in the data to create the baseline. So, basically, Elastic machine learning uses unsupervised learning to create the model that identifies the data anomaly. Once the baseline has been created, it can predict the future trend and can detect anomalies in the data. This way, once the model has been created, we can anticipate behavior for different reasons; for instance, if we are running a website and want to know how many users will be registered to our website in the next two years or how much traffic is expected in the coming weekend. In this way, machine learning can provide us with vital information just by reading our data, which is otherwise difficult to extract manually.

Machine learning features

Using Elastic Stack, we can create a full stack monitoring system that we can then use to monitor an application's performance and its databases, application logs, system logs, and packet details. This way, we can keep the complete information of the system. Since they all are connected through time series, we can easily check the root cause of any issue. This monitoring is very useful to get the details of every possible dataset, but how can we know whether something unusual is happening in the system and the reason behind this unusual behavior? Machine learning helps us find out about these types of details as it automatically finds anomalies in the data and shows us the details. There are many cases where machine learning can help us identify these issues. Some of these use cases are listed as follows:

- Identify whether there is an unusual drop or rise in application requests.
- Identify unusual network activity or user behavior.
- Catch the bottlenecks if the application is running slow.
- Get an idea about the normal behavior of the application.

- Detect whether there is any anomaly in the data.
- Identify the root cause of any problem in the application.
- Forecast future trends.

So, these are some use cases of machine learning in Elastic Stack, and we can solve some very crucial issues by using it. Now, we will cover the process of creating the machine learning jobs and to analyzing the results.

Creating machine learning jobs

Up until now, we have only discussed what machine learning is and its features. But to get the benefit of machine learning, we need to run the actual machine learning jobs. So, let's see how we can create machine learning jobs using our Elasticsearch data. We need to carry out the following steps to create a new machine learning job:

1. Click on the **Machine Learning** link from the left-hand menu of **Kibana**, which opens the **Job Management** screen. On this page, we can see a listing of the already-created jobs, if we have already created any, as shown in the following screenshot:

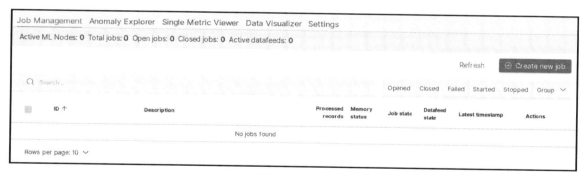

The preceding screenshot shows the **Job Management** page of **Machine Learning**.

2. To create a new job, we have to click on the **Create new job** button.

3. This opens the data selection page, where we can pick from the index or the saved search. We can select any index pattern (for example, **kibana_sample_data_flights**) from here. This will open the following screen:

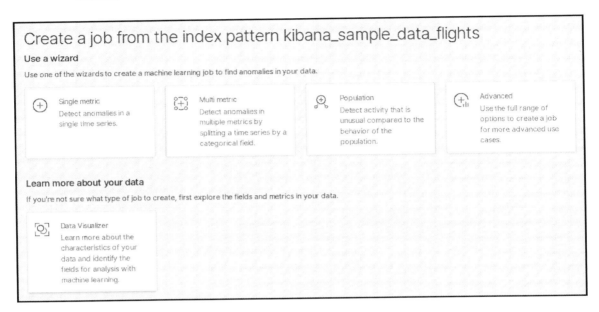

In the preceding screenshot, we can see the page, with different options to create a new machine learning job. We can create different types of jobs from here, such as **Single metric**, **Multi metric**, **Population**, or **Advanced**. If we are not sure about the data and fields on which we should apply a machine learning job, then we can use the **Data Visualizer** to help us understand our data before creating the machine learning job. The **Data Visualizer** helps us analyze our data and provides us with a view, using which we can easily understand our data.

Data visualizer

We can use the data visualizer to understand more about the data. This option tells us more about the characteristics of the data, through which we can identify the fields to apply for machine learning analysis. Here, we will take the example of *Kibana sample data flights* for executing the machine learning jobs. To understand more about this data, we can click on the **Data Visualizer** link from the wizard screen, which will open the data visualizer screen with the **Metrics** and **Fields** views of the flight data. The following screenshot shows the **Metrics** view of the page:

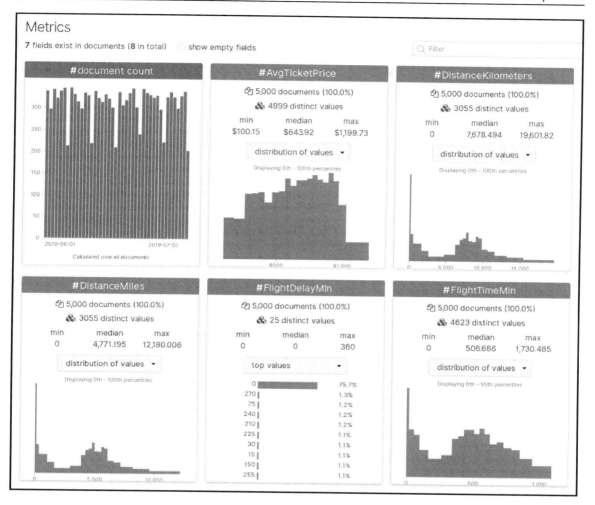

The preceding screenshot shows the first section of data visualization, which is **Metrics**. Here, we can see graphs for different metrics, such as document count, average ticket price, distance in kilometers, distance in miles, flight delay in minutes, flight time, and day of the week. These graphs provides us with a snapshot view for all of these metrics, such as minimum value, maximum value, median, distinct values, and total document count. Using a drop-down menu, we can change the graph view from the distribution of values to top values only.

In this way, using these metrics, we can get an idea about the data metrics that we are going to use for the machine learning job. Take a look at the following screenshot, which shows the field view part of the data visualizer page:

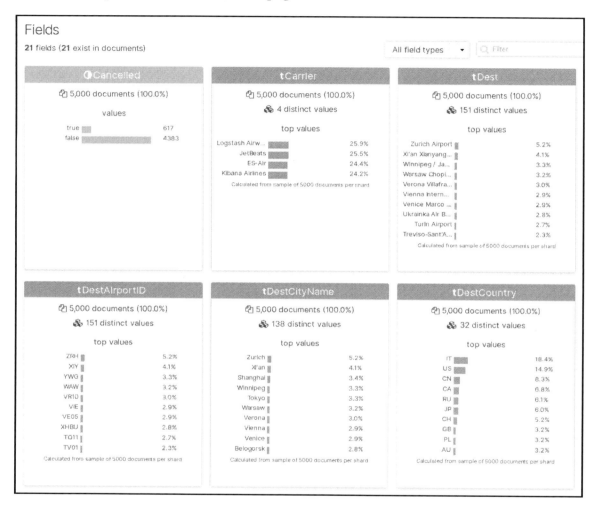

The preceding screenshot shows the **Field** section of the **Data Visualizer** page. Here, we can see different fields of the index, along with the different sets of values they contain. For each field, we have separate blocks where we can get the counts for total documents, distinct values, and top values. From this section, we can get the details for each field of the index. In this way, before running the actual machine learning job, it is good to view it through the **Data Visualizer** in order to understand and decide which fields we should apply the machine learning job to. Now, let's see how we can create single metric and multi-metric jobs.

Single metric jobs

In a single metric job, we have a single detector to define the type of analysis that will be performed and the field that will be analyzed. The detector defines the analysis type that is going to occur, such as maximum or average. So, basically, single metric jobs are those where we use a single field to run the machine learning job. Now, we are going to explain a practical example using machine learning.

Practical use case to explain machine learning

Here, we will take the example of *Kibana sample data flights* in order to execute the single metric job. This data comes with Elastic Stack by default, and we can easily download it using the Kibana UI. After we've done this, we refer to the following steps:

1. From the Wizard screen, we can click on the single metric box and set the **Aggregation** as **Max**, the **Field** as **FlightDelayMin**, and the **Bucket span** as **15m**. This will show the chart with the field metric displayed. If data hasn't been loaded, then click on the **Use full kibana_sample_data_flights data** button from the top-right corner of the page.

2. Next, add the job **Name** and **Description**. The following screenshot shows the job creation page:

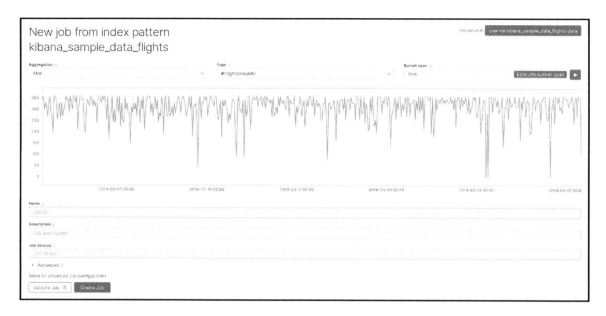

The preceding screenshot shows the single metric job creation page, where we are using the **Kibana_sample_data_flights** index pattern. We are aggregating the data using the maximum value of the **FlightDelayMin** field with a bracket span of 15 minutes. Below the text fields, we can see the graph, which is visualizing the configured aggregation. Below the graph, we can see the text boxes to add a **Name**, **Description**, and **Job Groups**, and so on before creating the job.

3. After filling in the details, we can click on the **Create job** button. This will create the job with a success message for the job's creation. Please refer to the following screenshot:

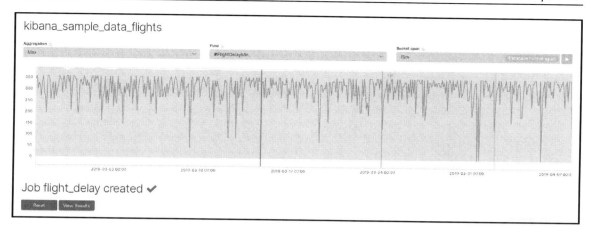

kibana_sample_data_flights

Job flight_delay created ✔

The preceding screenshot shows the confirmation page as the job is created. We can see the results by clicking on the **View Results** button. The following screenshot shows the results of the single metric machine learning job:

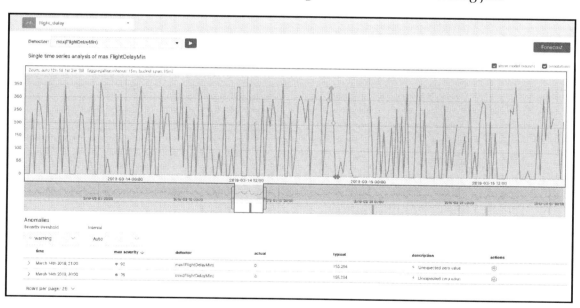

The preceding screenshot shows the single metric machine learning job results for the **Kibana_sample_data_flights** index pattern. Here, we can see the graph with different markers, which show unusual behavior in data. We can see two red marks in the graph; when we hover the mouse over these markers, it shows a popup with various information, such as anomaly score, multi-bucket impact, value, upper bounds, and lower bounds. We can see the tabular data for the anomalies in the following screenshot, which shows the time of anomaly, maximum severity, detector, actual value, typical value, description, and actions link. The rows of this tabular data are collapsible, so we can expand them by clicking on the arrow icon. In the expanded view, we can see other details as well, such as function, field name, job ID, multi-bucket impact, and probability, as shown in the following screenshot:

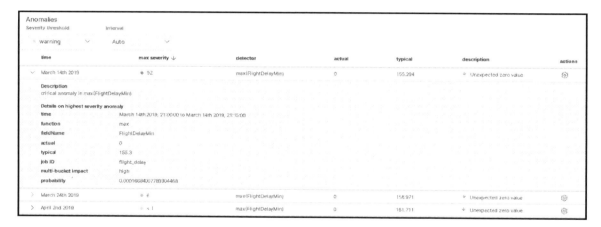

The preceding screenshot shows the expanded view of anomalies data, using which we can get the details of a particular anomaly. In the same way, we can view the details for all the markers of the graph, which denotes the unusual behavior of the data. This way, we can create a single metric machine learning job in Kibana and identify data anomalies.

Forecasting using machine learning

Except for anomaly detection, we can also use machine learning for future prediction. This is a very important feature, using which we can plan for the future. In Kibana machine learning, we can provide the days for which we want to generate the forecast. A forecast is a method whereby, reading the current data, we can predict future trends. To forecast trends, we need to click on the **Forecast** button above the graph on the right-hand side. It will open a popup to select the duration of the forecast, as shown in the following screenshot:

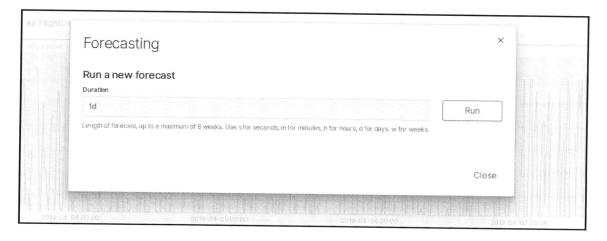

In the preceding screenshot, we can see the duration pop-up, where we can fill in the duration. Let's say we want to forecast the trend for the next five days. Here, we can fill **5d** in the textbox, which refers to five days, and then we can click on the **Execute** button. We can click on the **Close** button to close this window if we want to do so. Once we click on the **Execute** button, it will run the algorithm to process the result and show the future-predicted trends in a different color, which we can see in the following screenshot:

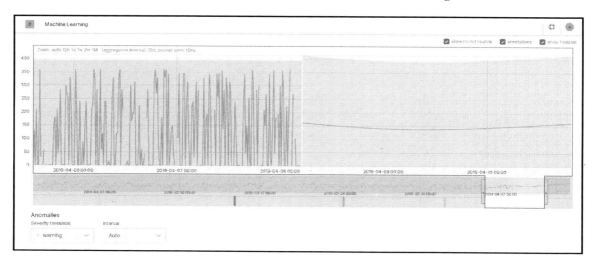

In the preceding screenshot, we can see the future trend graph with a surrounded area that is marked in a different color. This surrounded area shows us the possible variation in the prediction. The leaner the area is, the better the prediction can be. We can move the slider on the time range to change the graph view as per the selected time range. In the following screenshot, we can see the slider that can move in any direction. Based on its location, the main graph changes, and we can get the details for that time frame. The anomaly table will be displayed below the graph in order to gather the anomaly details. This way, we can generate the forecast on any Elasticsearch index data using the machine learning job. Using this forecast, we can get an idea about the future data trend, which is quite helpful for planning. For example, if we want to know about the sales of an e-commerce application and how it will grow, then by knowing that information before the actual crunch, we can plan for resources in a timely manner.

Multi-metric jobs

We can use multi-metric jobs when we have more than one detector as it is more efficient and easy to target multiple metrics of data rather than running multiple jobs on the same data for different metrics. So, basically, a multi-metric job is a machine learning job that we use to analyze multiple data points at the same time. Let's look at the same flight data example here as well and assume that we want to examine the average ticket price and flight duration of both. Here, we need to work with the **AvgTicketPrice** and **FlightTimeMin** fields. We can use both of them in a single multi-metric job.

To create a multi-metric job, refer to the following steps:

1. Click on the **Multi metric** box from the job selection wizard, which will open the following view:

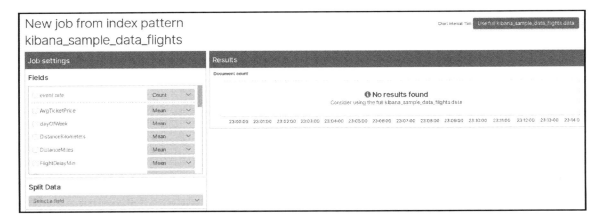

The preceding screenshot shows the page where you can create a multi-metric job. Here, we can click on the fields to add them for the job. We will select the **AvgTicketPrice** and **FlightTimeMin** fields.

2. Next, we can select the field to split the data. Here, we can pick the **Carrier** field to split the data points for different carriers. The **Bucket span** is provided to take the time interval, so here, we can add 15 minutes.

3. Finally, we need to provide the name and description of the job. Once everything is done, we can click on the **Create job** button to create the job. Please refer to the following screenshot:

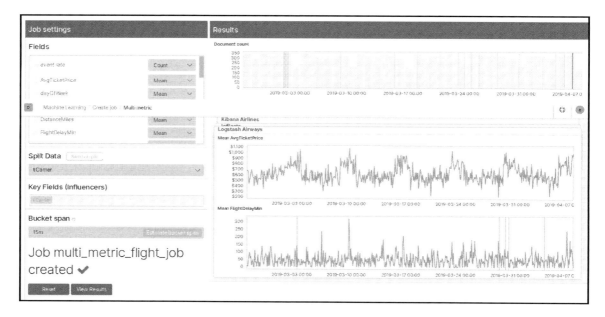

The preceding screenshot shows the job creation success page, where we can see a message stating **Job multi_metric_flight_job created**. We can also see the different graphs, which are stacked with different carrier names because we split the data using the carrier field.

4. To view the result, we can click on the **View Results** button. Please refer to the following screenshot:

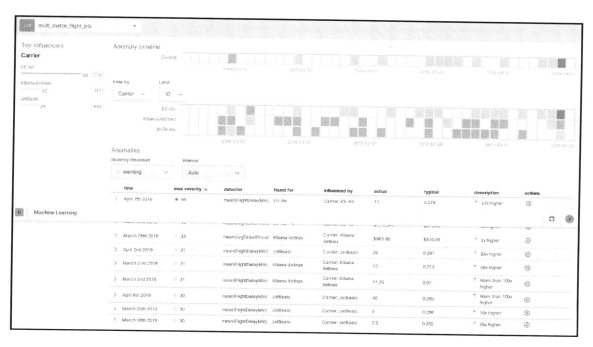

The preceding screenshot shows the multi-metric machine learning job result page; we can see the **Anomaly Explorer** view, where anomalies are shown as colored boxes. We can click on any colored box to see the details in the form of graphs and table that shows anomaly data. Here, we can see the blue, yellow, and red dots on the graph, for which details can be seen when we hover the cursor over them. Below the graph, we have a tabular representation of the anomalies with details such as typical value and actual value. On the left-hand side of the page, we can see the **Top Influencers**, under which we can see the carrier names with the maximum number of anomalies in descending order.

This way, we can analyze our data through single metric or multi-metric machine learning jobs. We can change the time duration using the time picker in the top right-hand corner to obtain the details for any specific duration. In the swim lane, we can click on any section to get more details about the anomalies, as shown in the following screenshot:

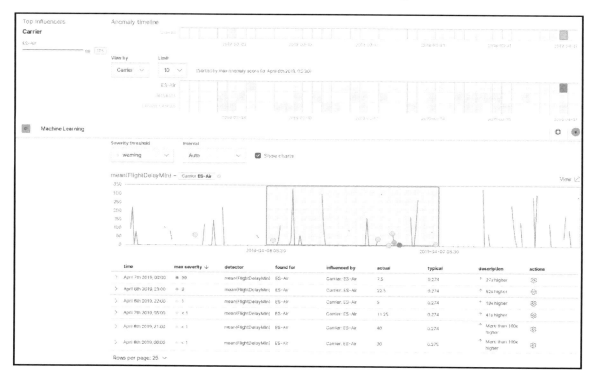

In this screenshot, I have clicked on the red block from the overall anomaly timeline, which has opened the anomaly detail graph, through which we can gain further insights about the anomaly. In the top right-hand corner of every graph, we have the **View** link, which opens the graph in the single metric viewer. From there, we can perform all of those operations that are supported in a single metric job, such as a forecast. Forecasting has been already explained in the *Single metric job* section.

Population jobs

A population job is a kind of job that works on population analysis, where we first need to analyze the data to identify the normal trend. Population analysis builds a profile of normal trends and then identifies whether an individual dataset behaves abnormally in comparison with the normal trend of the population.

To create a population job, refer to the following steps:

1. Click on the **Population** box from the job selection wizard, which will open the following view:

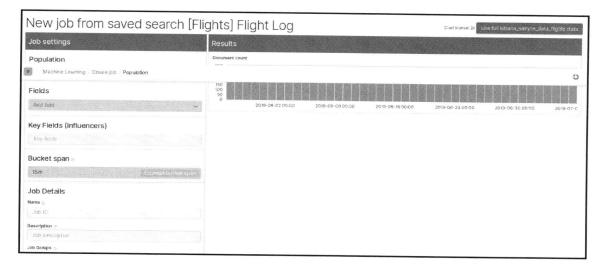

The preceding screenshot shows the job creation screen for a population type of machine learning job.

2. Now, we can add the **Job setting** parameters to run the job. For example, I have added the **Carrier** field for population after which, under fields, I have added the **FlightDelayMin** field. The **Bucket span** is set to **15m**. Then, I have provided the job name, description, and so on.

3. After filling in all of those details, we can click on the **Create job** button to create the job, as shown in the following screenshot:

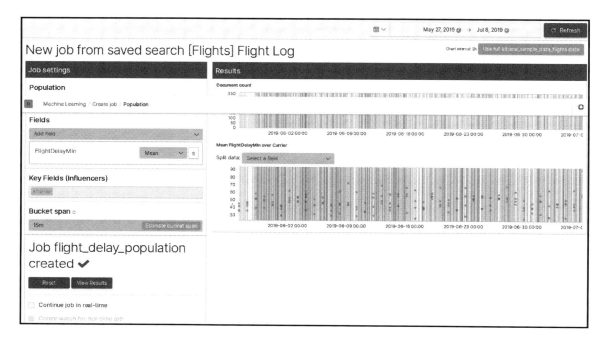

The preceding screenshot shows the job creation success page, where we can see a message stating **Job flight_delay_population created**. We can also see the different graphs, such as **Document count** and **Mean FlightDelayMin over Carrier**.

4. To view the result, we can click on the **View Results** button, as shown in the following screenshot:

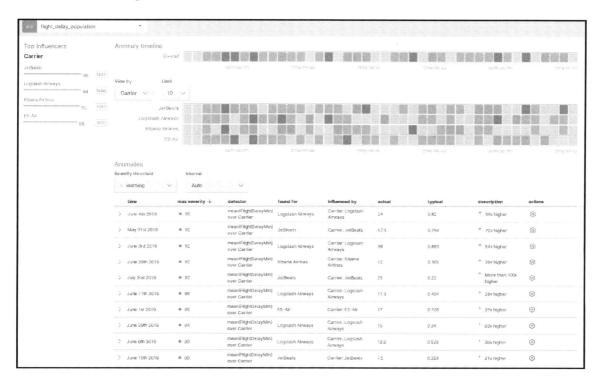

The preceding screenshot shows the same anomaly explorer view that we discussed in the previous type of jobs. Here, we have an anomaly timeline with different colored blocks and, below that, we can see the tabular view of various anomalies. This way, we can create and run a population machine learning job in Kibana.

In the same way, we can create an advanced job in Kibana. The advanced job provides us with more flexibility to select various options, but we can only use this job for advanced use cases. In an advanced job, along with job details, we can tweak analysis configuration and datafeeds, edit JSON files, and preview the data in the form of JSON files before creating the job.

In this way, we can create different types of machine learning jobs in Kibana in order to find data anomalies and forecast future trends.

Job management

Under job management, we can manage all the existing jobs through a job listing page. Once a job has been created, we can view it under the **Manage jobs** section of the **Machine Learning** page. To manage a job, we need to click on the **Job Management** tab on the **Machine Learning** page. This will open the following screen:

In the preceding screenshot, we can see the details about the job that we created earlier. On this page, we can see the following details:

- **ID**
- **Description**
- **Processed records**
- **Memory status**
- **Job state**
- **Datafeed state**
- **Latest timestamp**
- **Actions**

We can expand the view by clicking on the expand button before the job **ID** field to open the detailed view. On the detailed view, we have the following tabs:

- **Job settings**
- **Job config**
- **Datafeed**
- **Counts**
- **JSON**

- **Job messages**
- **Datafeed preview**
- **Forecast**

Job settings

Under the **Job settings** tab, we have a general section that shows us the **job_id**, **job_type**, **job_version**, **groups**, **description**, **create_time**, **finished_time**, **model_snapshot_retention_days**, **model_snapshot_id**, **results_index_name**, **state**, and **open_time** field details. The following screenshot shows the view of the **Job Settings** tab:

☐ ⌄ sd	flight_delay_job	10,396 ok

Job settings	Job config	Datafeed	Counts	JSON	Job messages	Datafeed preview	Forecasts	Annotations

General

job_id	sd
job_type	anomaly_detector
job_version	7.0.0
description	flight_delay_job
create_time	2019-06-08 15:16:49
finished_time	2019-06-08 15:18:43
model_snapshot_retention_days	1
model_snapshot_id	1559987229
results_index_name	shared
state	closed

The preceding screenshot shows the **Job settings** tab view, along with the different field names and their values.

Job config

Under the **Job config** tab, we can see the configuration that's used to run the machine learning job. It shows us the **Detectors**, **Analysis config (bucket_span, summary_count_field_name)**, **Analysis limits (model_memory_limit)**, and **Data description (time_field, time_format)** details.

The following screenshot shows the view of the **Job config** tab:

Job settings	Job config	Datafeed	Counts	JSON	Job messages	Datafeed preview	Forecasts	Annotations

Detectors   **Data description**

  max(FlightDelayMin)   time_field   timestamp

Analysis config   time_format   epoch_ms

  bucket_span   15m

  summary_count_field_name   doc_count

Analysis limits

  model_memory_limit   10mb

  categorization_examples_limit   4

The preceding screenshot shows the **Job config** tab view with different blocks, such as **Detectors**, **Analysis config**, **Analysis limits**, and **Data description**.

Datafeed

The **Datafeed** tab shows us different options, such as the **datafeed_id**, **job_id**, **query_delay**, **indices**, **query**, **aggregations**, **scroll_size**, **chunking_config**, **delayed_data_check_config**, and **state** fields. The following screenshot shows the view of the **Datafeed** tab:

Job settings	Job config	Datafeed	Counts	JSON	Job messages	Datafeed preview	Forecasts	Annotations

Datafeed

datafeed_id	datafeed-sd
job_id	sd
query_delay	85045ms
indices	kibana_sample_data_flights
query	{"bool":{"must":[{"match_all":{}}]}}
aggregations	{"buckets":{"date_histogram": {"field":"timestamp","interval":90000},"aggregations": {"FlightDelayMin":{"max": {"field":"FlightDelayMin"}},"timestamp":{"max": {"field":"timestamp"}}}}}
scroll_size	1000
chunking_config	{"mode":"manual","time_span":"90000000ms"}
delayed_data_check_config	{"enabled":true}
state	stopped

The preceding screenshot shows the **Datafeed** tab view, where we can see different field names and their values.

Counts

On the **Counts** tab, we can see two sections: **Counts** and **Model size stats**. Under **Counts**, we can see different fields such as **job_id, processed_record_count, processed_field_count, input_bytes, input_field_count, invalid_date_count, out_of_order_timestamp_count, empty_bucket_count, sparse_bucket_count, bucket_count, earliest_record_timestamp, latest_record_timestamp, last_data_time,** and **input_record_count**. Along with **Counts**, we have **Model size stats**, which includes **job_id, result_type, model_bytes, total_by_field_count, total_over_field_count, total_partition_field_count, memory_status, log_time,** and **timestamp**. The following screenshot shows a view of the **Counts** tab:

Job settings	Job config	Datafeed	Counts	JSON	Job messages	Datafeed preview	Forecasts	Annotations

Counts		Model size stats	
job_id	sd	job_id	sd
processed_record_count	10,396	result_type	model_size_stats
processed_field_count	20,792	model_bytes	39.2 KB
input_bytes	644.9 KB	total_by_field_count	3
input_field_count	20,792	total_over_field_count	0
invalid_date_count	0	total_partition_field_count	2
missing_field_count	0	bucket_allocation_failures_count	0
out_of_order_timestamp_count	0	memory_status	ok
empty_bucket_count	199	log_time	2019-06-08 15:18:43
sparse_bucket_count	0	timestamp	2019-07-08 05:00:00
bucket_count	4,031		
earliest_record_timestamp	2019-05-27 05:30:00		
latest_record_timestamp	2019-07-08 05:16:01		
last_data_time	2019-06-08 15:17:06		
latest_empty_bucket_timestamp	2019-07-08 05:00:00		
input_record_count	10,396		

The preceding screenshot shows the **Counts** tab view, along with the **Counts** and **Model size stats** options.

JSON

The **JSON** tab view displays the JSON data of complete job-related details, which we can copy from here in JSON format. The following screenshot shows a view of the **JSON** tab:

The preceding screenshot shows the **JSON** tab view. Here, we can see the machine learning job description in JSON format.

Job messages

The **Job messages** tab shows the time-wise log messages for a machine learning job. These are quite helpful as they provide us with the log messages, through which we can understand the complete flow of the job creation. The following screenshot shows a view of the **Job messages** tab:

	Job settings	Job config	Datafeed	Counts	JSON	Job messages	Datafeed preview	Forecasts	Annotations

	Time	Node	Message
⚠	2019-06-08 15:16:48	▨▨▨▨(LPTP03 05	Job created
⚠	2019-06-08 15:16:50	KELLGGNLPTP03 05	Opening job on node [{KELLGGNLPTP0305}{OsuaWgbGQd2KXbWE3ENfEgjXxU2BKKqSBmtIEWJsIMaQQ}{127.0.0.1}{127.0.0.1:9300}{ml.machine_memory=16709136384, xpack.installed=true, ml.max_open_jobs=20}]
⚠	2019-06-08 15:16:50	KELLGGNLPTP03 05	Loading model snapshot [N/A], job latest_record_timestamp [N/A]
⚠	2019-06-08 15:16:51	KELLGGNLPTP03 05	Starting datafeed [datafeed-sd] on node [{KELLGGNLPTP0305}{OsuaWgbGQd2KXbWE3ENfEgjXxU2BKKqSBmtIEWJsIMaQQ}{127.0.0.1}{127.0.0.1:9300}{ml.machine_memory=16709136384, xpack.installed=true, ml.max_open_jobs=20}]
⚠	2019-06-08 15:16:51	KELLGGNLPTP03 05	Datafeed started (from: 2019-05-27T00:00:00.000Z to: 2019-07-07T23:50:12.001Z) with frequency [450000ms]
⚠	2019-06-08 15:17:08	KELLGGNLPTP03 05	Datafeed lookback completed
⚠	2019-06-08 15:17:09	KELLGGNLPTP03 05	Datafeed stopped
⚠	2019-06-08 15:17:09	KELLGGNLPTP03 05	Job is closing
⚠	2019-06-08 15:18:41	KELLGGNLPTP03 05	Opening job on node [{KELLGGNLPTP0305}{OsuaWgbGQd2KXbWE3ENfEgjXxU2BKKqSBmtIEWJsIMaQQ}{127.0.0.1}{127.0.0.1:9300}{ml.machine_memory=16709136384, xpack.installed=true, ml.max_open_jobs=20}]

Rows per page: 10 ∨

The preceding screenshot shows the **Job messages** tab view, where we can see different messages related to jobs with times.

Datafeed preview

The **Datafeed preview** tab view provides us with the JSON view for the aggregated document data. The following screenshot shows a view of the **Datafeed preview** tab:

Job settings	Job config	Datafeed	Counts	JSON	Job messages	Datafeed preview	Forecasts	Annotations

```
15        "doc_count": 1
16    },
17  ▾ {
18        "FlightDelayMin": 0,
19        "timestamp": 1558917211000,
20        "doc_count": 1
21    },
22  ▾ {
23        "FlightDelayMin": 300,
24        "timestamp": 1558917411000,
25        "doc_count": 2
26    },
27  ▾ {
28        "FlightDelayMin": 180,
29        "timestamp": 1558917848000,
30        "doc_count": 2
31    },
32  ▾ {
33        "FlightDelayMin": 0,
34        "timestamp": 1558918029000,
35        "doc_count": 1
36    },
37  ▾ {
38        "FlightDelayMin": 0,
39        "timestamp": 1558918728000,
40        "doc_count": 1
41    },
42  ▾ {
43        "FlightDelayMin": 15,
44        "timestamp": 1558918911000,
45        "doc_count": 1
46    },
47  ▾ {
48        "FlightDelayMin": 300,
49        "timestamp": 1558919300000,
50        "doc_count": 2
51    }
52  ]
```

The preceding screenshot shows the **Datafeed preview** tab view, where we can see the JSON data with aggregation.

Forecasts

The **Forecasts** tab view shows us the list of forecasts that we have generated under the machine learning job. It provides us with the creation date, duration, status, memory size, processing time, and expiry date, and so on, along with a link to view the forecast page, as shown in the following screenshot:

The preceding screenshot shows the **Forecasts** tab view, where we can get a list of all the forecasts we have created so far.

Summary

In this chapter, we covered the machine learning feature of Kibana. We started with an introduction to Elastic machine learning and explained various features of machine learning using Kibana. After that, we explored machine learning job creation, where we started with the data visualizer to explain how we can use it to understand data before running the actual job. We started with machine learning jobs with single metric job creation and analysis, before we moved on to multi-metric and population job creation and analysis. We also covered forecasting using machine learning, whereby we can predict future trends and plan accordingly.

Other Books You May Enjoy

If you enjoyed this book, you may be interested in these other books by Packt:

Learning Elastic Stack 7.0 - Second Edition
Pranav Shukla, Sharath Kumar M N

ISBN: 978-1-78995-439-5

- Install and configure an Elasticsearch architecture
- Solve the full-text search problem with Elasticsearch
- Discover powerful analytics capabilities through aggregations using Elasticsearch
- Build a data pipeline to transfer data from a variety of sources into Elasticsearch for analysis
- Create interactive dashboards for effective storytelling with your data using Kibana

Kibana 7 Quick Start Guide
Anurag Srivastava

ISBN: 978-1-78980-403-4

- Explore how Logstash is configured to fetch CSV data
- Understand how to create index patterns in Kibana
- Become familiar with how to apply filters on data
- Discover how to create ML jobs
- Explore how to analyze APM data from APM agents

Leave a review - let other readers know what you think

Please share your thoughts on this book with others by leaving a review on the site that you bought it from. If you purchased the book from Amazon, please leave us an honest review on this book's Amazon page. This is vital so that other potential readers can see and use your unbiased opinion to make purchasing decisions, we can understand what our customers think about our products, and our authors can see your feedback on the title that they have worked with Packt to create. It will only take a few minutes of your time, but is valuable to other potential customers, our authors, and Packt. Thank you!

Index

Made in the USA
San Bernardino, CA
29 August 2019